CAN YOU AFFORD TO DIE?

CAN YOU AFFORD TO DIE?

HOW TO NAVIGATE A FAMILY DEATH & CONTROL THE COST OF A FUNERAL

A Complete End-of-Life Planning Guide

CLARE ANTHONY

Note that the information contained within this document is for educational and reference purposes only and should not be construed as professional advice. The content within this book has been derived from various sources cited within.

Every effort has been made to present accurate, up-to-date, and reliable information. Statistics have been cited, and funeral pricing has been derived from price lists obtained by the author, which are accurate at the time of publication. Any omissions or errors are unintentional.

In light of the complex and unique circumstances of every death and each family's financial situation, readers acknowledge that the information in this book is presented for your consideration but is not intended to replace financial, legal or post-death advice. This book includes funeral planning and financial information that may not be right for you, and no warranties of any kind are declared or implied.

The publisher and the author expressly disclaim any responsibility for any loss or risk incurred as a consequence of the application of the contents of this book. By reading this document, the reader agrees that under no circumstances is the author responsible for any direct or indirect losses incurred as a result of the use of the information contained within this document, including, but not limited to, errors, omissions, or inaccuracies. Please consult a licensed financial, legal, or funeral professional to verify that the information herein is appropriate for your personal situation.

For information or permissions, contact
Hildegard's Creations, LLC
P.O. Box 590654
Houston, TX 77259-0654

Clare.Anthony.HC@gmail.com.

ISBN: 978-1-963193-00-8 eBook
ISBN: 978-1-963193-02-2 Print book

10 9 8 7 6 5 4 3 2

Contents

Preface

What This Book Can Do for You and How to Maximize Its Use

Since this is a guidebook, it does not have to be read sequentially to be valuable.

This book is written for four different readers.

Reader 1: The person who has just experienced a death. Chapters 1-13 are filled with information regarding everything you need to know about the complexities of navigating a death and funeral. Being aware of this information before you need it is the best way to be proactive and save money when death arrives.

Reader 2: The person who knows that a death is imminent. This time is a sobering realization for immediate family members, but it can also give you valuable time to avert a financial disaster. You may discover that your loved one has no plan for their passing or money saved for even the simplest funeral. You may discover that they do not have a will or beneficiaries set up. Knowing what is in this book during this time can give you valuable insights regarding questions to ask, time to set up medical directives or write a will, and query the location of valuable paperwork, like passwords, deeds, financial documents, or insurance policies.

Reader 3: There is no death on your horizon, but you want to know the possible financial fallout of a family death. It is not widely discussed, but the cost of the funeral can financially destabilize a family. This invoice must be paid within a week, even before your loved one is cremated or buried, and the cost can be $10,000 or more. If the death is sudden, traumatic, or unexpected, a family can be upended for months or even years. If you are the brave person who picked up this very uncomfortable book to determine the consequences that a death may have on your family, begin with the sobering information in Chapters 14 and 15. It may make a significant difference in your future by motivating you to make a plan.

Reader 4: Any person who could incur responsibilities in the aftermath of a family death. Spouses, adult children, parents, or siblings of a deceased family member can be impacted financially and legally as a result of a death. Is it possible you could become a caretaker or parent overnight?

If you are the one who may be left to pick up the pieces, read Chapters 14-19 first to prepare yourself for difficult conversations. These chapters suggest tools to mitigate the financial aftermath of death, including writing a will, purchasing life insurance, and creating end-of-life medical documents to protect your family from financial chaos after the loss of a family member. Death causes both emotional and financial stress for families. The emotional upheaval is inevitable, but this book provides tools to mitigate the financial fallout.

Your courage to read this book before you need it may give your family peace of mind in the wake of the unthinkable.

It has occurred to me that I probably have not written the next best seller. Rather, I've written *a book nobody wants to read.* But, if there is a chance that you or one of your loved ones might die, this book contains information that you may not even know you need.

So why did I move forward writing this book? For over four decades as a church musician, I helped hundreds of families plan funerals for their loved ones. Each family I met had a story. I attended each funeral and listened to tearful eulogies describing real people. I saw firsthand what a hardship death can be. Encountering families during this vulnerable moment of grief drew me to focus on all of the challenges facing that family. This experience was a profound personal privilege for me.

The first thirteen chapters of this book present details of what you will face after the death of a family member. It will give you an inside view of all aspects of planning a funeral, and you will learn about the legal protections that the Federal Trade Commission affords you during this time. This book also provides important information you will need to navigate a death and presents cost-saving alternatives to the traditional funeral.

The remaining chapters help you assess whether or not you can afford to die by uncovering the real costs of a funeral and presenting the financial consequences of this expense from a consumer's perspective rather than that of a salesperson for end-of-life plans. You will be provided examples of funeral costs from around the country. This book will teach you how to proactively shop for funeral goods and services either at the time of death or in advance. It also discusses the importance of acquiring *General Price Lists* before you commit to a funeral home, warns you of funeral homes that try to withhold them, and, most importantly, gives you the tools to decipher them.

In summary, you need this book if :

- you don't consider yourself a wealthy person.
- you don't know how much funerals cost or how you would pay for one.
- you don't know that you can shop for funeral homes.
- you don't know how cemeteries function.

> ***But most of all, you need this book if a multi-thousand-dollar expense payable next week would significantly reduce your savings or add credit card debt.***

If you can't bring yourself to read this book right now, I hope you will keep it on a bookshelf for the future, or at least keep it for a friend in their hour of need—or God forbid—for your family in case they lose *you*. If this topic is too stressful for you to think about right now, may I suggest you ease into it by reading just one chapter at a time.

> ***I assure you that the only thing scary about this book is not knowing what's in it.***

In fact, reading *Can You Afford to Die?* now will give you the gift of hindsight before a tragedy arrives. It may help you see the urgency of making a plan now to ensure your family remains financially whole after a death.

> ***In conclusion, let me ask one simple question. How much money would you need in your bank account to comfortably handle a $20,000 cash purchase next week without considering that amount a significant withdrawal?***

After reading these words, I ask, are you prepared if death is on your calendar today and include a follow-up question: Once you've seen the big picture, what will you do about it while you still have time? *Your loved ones are counting on you.*

Chapter 1

Funeral—Memorial Service— Celebration of Life? Where Do I Begin?

- *A funeral can be either religious or secular and is usually held within days of death, while a memorial service or celebration of life is sometimes held weeks or months later.*
- *The days following a death are important gathering times for immediate and extended family and friends of the deceased, providing consolation for the bereaved and closure for the family.*
- *It celebrates a deceased person's life and contributions to their family, friends, and community.*

Once you begin to process the news that you have just received, the word funeral will be foremost in your mind, but what *is* a funeral, and how do you start planning? Here are the four most common options:

- A **funeral** is a service with either a body or cremains present.
- A **memorial service** is a service without a body or cremains present.
- A **celebration of life** can be a religious or secular service, either with or without cremains present.
- A **graveside service** is a service that is held at the cemetery at the time of burial of a body or cremains.

It may surprise you, but these celebrations are primarily for the living. A funeral is a structured service that draws together a person's family, friends, and colleagues to celebrate the life, love, accomplishments, and often the faith of this unique individual. Death, especially a tragic or unexpected one, seems to stop or suspend time for those closest to the deceased. The act of planning a funeral slowly restarts time by allowing a family to share the company of their relatives and friends, return to their roots, and reconnect with their past for a few days. Spending time with family grounds those most impacted by the death. It cushions the loss and transitions them back into the present and the new reality of life without their loved one.

> ***Planning a funeral or any end-of-life celebration, difficult though it may be, is a virtual buffer between the past and the future.***

During these days, generations gather to look back and reminisce, share pictures, recall memories, and find ways to memorialize and honor this special individual called husband, wife, mother, father, daughter, son, brother, sister, cousin, grandmother, grandfather, aunt, or uncle. It summons those who care most about you to listen, share stories, and offer consolation and comfort to you and each other.

A funeral service should be a celebration of a person's life. It serves a dual function of publicly commemorating and honoring your loved one and providing a structure in which mourners can say their final goodbyes and collectively begin the grief process, which may take months, if not years to pass through.

This celebration can be a **religious service** in a church or funeral home, with prayer, Scripture, music, and tributes, or a **secular service** at a funeral home or other venue with inspirational thoughts, music, and testimonials. In the past, funerals have been held within a week of death, and if the death has been unexpected or the deceased is to be buried, most families choose to hold the funeral within that time frame. Other families choose this timeline for closure and to return to the demands of the living.

Two time-sensitive decisions that need to be made quickly

1. Will you bury or cremate your loved one?
2. Will you choose a full-service funeral home or a direct cremation facility?

These two decisions, discussed at length in the next two chapters, will determine the course of the next few days.

In most states, you are required to use a funeral director to arrange for the final disposition of your loved one's remains, but there is no legal requirement to use a funeral director to plan a service or to have a funeral service at all.

Where do I begin? What needs to be done after you learn of a family death?

If you have just purchased this book, you may have recently experienced a death, so my first recommendation is to take a breath—and now take another—and remember that the people who will walk these next few days with you are family. Be gentle and recognize the glass-half-full aspects of their personalities. They, too, are grieving, so try to ensure that these relationships do not get fractured during this time. Listen, be respectful, and be kind to one another!

An effective tool during this time is to keep people busy. There is much to do; some of it is creative, and some is more pragmatic. Don't be afraid to delegate. I've given you the CHECKLIST in *Chapter* 5 so that from the first moment, you can get to work using the talents and gifts of each family member. This will allow everyone to participate in the process and feel valued.

Here are some critical tasks to assign:

- Notify a church, synagogue, or other fraternal organization to inform friends of your loved one's passing.
- Find a loving home for any pets left behind.
- If your loved one lived alone, ensure their home, property, and vehicle are secure.
- Determine if there are any pre-paid funeral arrangements or a pre-purchased cemetery plot.
- Has your loved one outlined any wishes for their funeral service?
- Search for a life insurance or burial policy.
- Does any family member have a joint checking account with the deceased to pay for final expenses?
- Choose family members to write an obituary and a eulogy
- If appropriate, contact the landlord to determine the terms of the lease.
- If appropriate, notify your loved one's employer and determine if any benefits are available.
- Gather family photos for a memorial presentation, a head shot of the deceased for the service, and memorial cards.

Will the funeral be a religious service?

Most people feel lost when confronted with planning a funeral. Those with a religious affiliation can rely on their religious tradition to guide them through the process. Otherwise, only those who have previously been through funeral planning know where to begin, and those walking through it for the first time or those who have no religious affiliation tend to rely entirely on the funeral director's guidance. This can be a very costly choice, as will be discussed in subsequent chapters.

> **Consider this:**
> ***I sometimes saw clashes among family members regarding whether a funeral should be in a church or at a funeral home. A good rule of thumb is this: If your deceased loved one belonged to a church community, the funeral should be held in that faith tradition without exception.***

This end-of-life celebration is about completing your loved one's life cycle within their belief system. Do not let your differing beliefs nor your personal discomfort with these beliefs derail this tribute to your loved one. On the other hand, if your loved one did not have any religious affiliation, then all options are open.

Your family

Someone is the first to get the news, and now you will be in constant contact with siblings, cousins, distant aunts and uncles, neighbors, and family friends. Life is complicated these days, and families may be spread worldwide. If there is to be a funeral or gathering of some sort, you will need to coordinate the travel schedules of your family members. Be patient; some may have to notify their superiors and hand off important time-sensitive tasks to colleagues. Life does go on even though it has stopped for your family.

Gather family photos and mementos

This is an excellent time to look for family photos for a video presentation. Identify a unique image to enlarge and use as a portrait of your loved one for the visitation and funeral/memorial service. This picture will also be used for memorial cards or a funeral program. You may also gather other significant personal items, such as military honors or medals; you'll be surprised at how many times you will need these. Viewing old photos and treasures is important to both grieving and healing. Take time to reminisce and tell stories. Laugh and cry together. This can be a healing time to deepen family relationships, especially among adult siblings and extended family.

Take time to grieve

Your relationship with your loved one is unique to *you*. Take time to be with your thoughts. There is an empty hole in your heart. Emotions can be raw and erupt without warning. There is no template for grieving and no express passage through it. It is normal to have both positive and negative emotions after your loved one's passing. You may experience sadness, anger, or even guilt about what could have been different in your relationship. You may need to spend time alone to process your emotions, but staying connected to your friends and other family is also important during this time.

There are many ways to honor your loved one, but let's start with the most expensive one— a traditional funeral.

$ *The dollar sign icons indicate that you can expect to pay for each of these items or services when planning a traditional funeral.*

When a person dies, **$** the body is picked up from the hospital, nursing home, hospice facility, morgue, or other place of death by a van and delivered to your chosen funeral home. The funeral director will then ask what your wishes are. Do you want your loved one to be **$** embalmed and buried or **$** cremated? You are shown **$** caskets for burial or **$** cremation containers and **$** urns based on your decision. If your loved one is to be buried, the funeral director will ask you to choose clothing for them.

If you have chosen burial, either of a body or cremated remains, the funeral director will ask where you would like your loved one buried and show you **$** burial vaults and **$** grave liners. Which cemetery would you like to use? Do you have a **$** cemetery plot? You will be informed of cemetery policies, regulations, and costs. The funeral director may have this information for you or send you to the cemetery to discuss your wishes with their personnel.

You will be asked **$** what kind of service you would like—religious or secular— where you would like it to be —**$** a church, **$** a funeral home, or **$** a venue—and will there be a **$** wake/viewing/visitation. The funeral director will send you home to gather information for the death certificate. Think about **$** how many death certificates you would like. Ten to twenty might be a good number to start.

Next, you will be sent to gather photos. The funeral director will ask you to enlarge a photo or two of your loved one to display at the funeral. Do you want a **$** memorial video presentation for the visitation, funeral, or reception? Choose the photos you would like to use.

It's time to gather information and write an obituary for publication on the funeral home website or to be placed in your **$** local newspaper. Next, it's time to think about a eulogy. Who will write it, and who will deliver it?

Do you want **$** flowers, and who will provide them? And yes, the funeral director can offer assistance for the **$** arrangements for the funeral home or church or a **$** funeral arrangement for the casket.

Consider if you wish to ask friends to send flowers or prefer to have their donations directed to a favorite charity. Do you need financial assistance to pay for final expenses? If so, you may choose to request donations via crowdfunding platforms.

If the funeral is at the **$** funeral home, they will ask how you would like to structure it. Who will lead the service? Will **$** a member of the clergy be invited to preside? Or would you like the **$** funeral director to do that for you? Will there be speakers? Will someone deliver a eulogy, or will you invite several people to speak? Do you want **$** music, live or recorded, Scripture, or inspirational poems or passages? Please choose those.

If the funeral or viewing is at a **$** church, you will be sent off to meet with the staff or clergy. In this setting, the service format may be more structured based on your selected religious tradition. You will be guided to choose Scripture and **$** music. You may also be asked to select family or friends to read Scripture or sing.

You will be asked if you would like to **$** gather at the funeral home for one last viewing of your loved one before the funeral service begins. Do you want **$** transportation to the church from the funeral home and from the **$** church to the cemetery? Do you want a **$** graveside service, and who will preside—the **$** funeral director, a family member, or **$** clergy?

These questions will be addressed within twenty-four hours of learning of your loved one's death. In a traditional funeral timeline, you then have another twenty-four to thirty-six hours to perform all these tasks, and at some time between days three and seven, it will all come together as a funeral service. This outline has been followed for decades.

For some, this timeline can be difficult to execute in our ever-more challenging world with family members who may live or do business in far-reaching corners of the country or the world. Gathering your relatives and planning a funeral in seventy-two hours or even a week may not be possible.

The good news is that it is the twenty-first century, and many old norms have been broken. For instance, if your loved one is to be cremated, there is no urgency in planning a funeral. Families may wait weeks or even months to have a memorial service or celebration of life, possibly in another location. Now, you can have a service honoring your loved one whenever and wherever it is appropriate for your family.

Are there times when you may choose not to have a funeral at the time of death?

Yes, and the reasons for this choice can be:

- You might not be able to afford the cost of a funeral at this time. You do have to bury or cremate your loved one within days of death, but you may choose Direct Cremation or Immediate Burial if you do not want the expense of a funeral at the time of death.
- The logistics of gathering your family may be too complicated at this time.
- You may not feel you can adequately prepare a celebration of your loved one's life while you are grieving.
- Your loved one wanted to have their ashes scattered or be buried in a different location which may require some planning.
- It might not be possible for everyone to attend at the time of death, and you do not want to leave anyone out.
- Your loved one stated that they did not want a funeral.

Chapter 5 provides a CHECKLIST, an overview of planning a funeral. The details of how to accomplish each task are presented in *Chapters* 9-14. With this CHECKLIST, you can look behind the curtain and see the big picture before starting to plan so that you can enlist family and friends to assist you by giving each an assignment that best suits their skills. For some, this CHECKLIST will provide an outline with enough information to design a funeral themselves. If you choose, you can use this information to plan your service without the assistance of a funeral director.

Summary

Funerals are an important means of emotional closure. By gathering immediate and extended family and friends and sharing stories, the living remember and honor this unique person, acknowledge their loss, and begin the grieving process.

Unfortunately, the loss of a loved one is also a financial matter. If you have suffered an unexpected death and you choose the customary path for a funeral, the funeral expenses may signal the beginning of significant financial stress for your family. Armed with the information in this book, you can be proactive rather than reactive in approaching the funeral planning process, either with or without a funeral director. Thus, you may save hundreds or even thousands of dollars by making careful, informed, and deliberate choices while creating a dignified, memorable send-off for your loved one.

There is no right or wrong way to plan a funeral. You must use a funeral director for the disposition of remains, but how you honor your loved one is entirely up to you.

Notes

Chapter 2

Burial, Cremation, or Donation to Science?

- *Most people assume cremation is less costly than burial, but this is often not the case. To verify this, you must gather and analyze General Price Lists and read all the fine print.*
- *The first decision you must make after a death is not which funeral home you would like to use but whether you will cremate or bury your loved one.*
- *Hopefully, your loved one has made their wishes known before death.*
- *Donating your body to science is rarely considered. Still, it can benefit both society through research and training and your family financially by reducing or eliminating the cost of a funeral and a burial.*

> **STOP! You Are Now at a Critical Decision Point!**
>
> ***The first decision you should consider is whether you want to bury or cremate your loved one. However, the first question you will be asked is: "Which funeral home would you like us to call?"***

Why is the order of these two decisions so critical?

What if I told you that the price of your funeral if you choose cremation vs. burial before choosing a funeral home could range from $800 to $5,000, and if you choose a funeral home before you decide on cremation or burial, the price of your funeral could range between $4,000 and $20,000. Would that get your attention?

Putting the cart before the horse!

Deciding to bury or cremate your loved one before choosing a funeral home allows you to choose a direct cremation facility rather than a full-service funeral home, but if you choose a funeral home first, you forfeit that option. Understand that if you choose a direct cremation facility, *that business becomes your funeral home.* These facilities employ licensed funeral directors and will fulfill all of your post-death needs, including moving your loved one from the place of death, securing permits, filing the death certificate, and returning your loved one's cremains to you.

> **It is essential for your family to choose burial or cremation before you select a facility.**

Now consider what could happen if you select a funeral home immediately after you are notified of the death.

Those who are grieving are emotionally overwhelmed and have difficulty making even simple decisions. But more importantly, they are unfamiliar with what a funeral director does and are so overwhelmed by the numerous steps involved in planning a funeral that they prefer to go on autopilot. They passively rely on the funeral director to take care of everything during this difficult time.

Once you name a funeral home, the funeral director has obtained your implied consent to move your loved one to his facility. This triggers a $500–$1,100 transportation fee and the non-refundable *Basic Services Fee*, which can be $1,800–$5,700 depending on where you live. Understand that the only thing that has happened at this point is the transportation of your loved one from the place of death to the funeral home. From this moment on, after accruing these fees, it is highly unlikely that you will make another choice. So, when you answer the funeral home question first, the funeral director is quite sure that he has secured your business.

Here are options that you might not know exist

You may not know that funeral homes offer less expensive, no-frills options for cremation and burial. This allows you to use the funeral home for cremation or burial but not use them to plan a funeral. You can now plan a visitation, funeral, and reception at your house of worship or a venue, possibly at a reduced cost. To take advantage of these options and present them to a funeral director, you must be aware that they exist and get a copy of the *General Price List* from the funeral home to discuss the cost of a *Direct Cremation* or *Immediate Burial*.

The *Funeral Rule*

It is important now to pause and briefly describe the *Funeral Rule*, which will be discussed at length in Chapter 6, but for our purposes here, it is important to know that the Federal Trade Commission has regulated the funeral industry since 1984.

The *Funeral Rule* describes important rights that you may not know you have but that the funeral home must abide by. Knowing these rights and proactively approaching the funeral director as an informed consumer may prevent misunderstandings and ensure transparent pricing. Throughout the next few chapters, I will be quoting the *Funeral Rule* in the sections called "The FTC says." as I refer to some of the protections it affords. These quotes will also serve to reinforce the information being presented.

Do I have to use a funeral home to plan a funeral after my family loses a loved one?

> **The FTC says:** "*Many people don't realize that in most states, they are not legally required to use a funeral home to plan and conduct a funeral. However, because they have little experience with the many details and legal requirements involved and may be emotionally distraught when it's time to make the plans, they find the service of a professional funeral home to be a comfort.*"
> https://consumer.ftc.gov/articles/choosing-funeral-provider

I would be willing to wager that a majority of the population feels they must choose a funeral home immediately after a family death, and so are psychologically conditioned to respond to the question: "Which funeral home would you like us to call?"

How did these questions get reversed?

The funeral industry has taken it upon itself to blend its legal contract with your state to your family's desire to celebrate your loved one. There are actually three important post-death actions:

1. Retrieval and storage of your loved one's body.
2. Disposition of their remains by burial or cremation.
3. Celebrating your loved one's life.

The first two actions require a funeral director, but the third one does not. To say this differently, someone needs to retrieve and store a deceased body, someone needs to maintain a chain of custody of the deceased until it is safely buried or cremated, and someone needs to record the death and report it to the state. These are the official roles of the funeral director, and after he fulfills these obligations to the state, it sets up a perfect scenario for him to convince you that *his* funeral home is best suited to assist with all of your needs in the days following your loss. So, once you contact a funeral director, it is very difficult to reverse course after your loved one is moved to his facility.

This is a good time to discuss the terminology found on General Price Lists

Before proceeding any further, let's discuss the terminology needed to understand the material presented. Here is some of the funeral industry vocabulary used in this book.

The *General Price List* (GPL)

The FTC, under the *Funeral Rule*, mandates that every funeral home in the U.S. create a *General Price List* that shows the cost of all goods and services they offer. The funeral director determines the pricing and format of the price list, but the *Funeral Rule* mandates that the GPL must incorporate the cost of all goods and services common to the funeral industry.

The list below is incomplete, but it gives you an idea of the services and prices that you will find on every GPL:

- Embalming or refrigeration of a body
- Body preparation for a visitation
- Use of facilities and staff for a visitation, funeral, or graveside service
- Use of vehicles to transport a body to the funeral home, church, crematorium, and cemetery
- Direct Cremation
- Immediate Burial
- Caskets and urns
- Printed materials and flowers

It should be noted that two other price lists must be considered if you are having a funeral with a burial: the *Casket Price List* and the *Burial Container Price List*. These terms are self-explanatory.

The *Basic Services Fee*

> **The FTC says:** "*The Funeral Rule allows funeral providers to charge a Basic Services Fee that customers have to pay. It includes services that are common to all funerals, regardless of the specific arrangement.*" https://consumer.ftc.gov/articles/ftc-funeral-rule

This fee is a cost *of doing business* fee and may be referred to as a *non-declinable* fee. The FTC requires that the funeral home disclose this fee on the GPL, and it includes the arrangements conference, planning the funeral, securing the necessary permits, filing the death certificate, preparing notices, and coordinating the cemetery or crematory arrangements. https://www.ftc.gov/business-guidance/resources/complying-funeral-rule#the-general-price-list

---

The FTC says: " *A fee for our basic services and overhead will be added to the total cost of the funeral arrangements you select. (This fee is already included in our charges for direct cremations, immediate burials, and forwarding or receiving remains.)*" https://www.ftc.gov/business-guidance/resources/complying-funeral-rule#the-general-price-list

---

An Advocate

The term *Advocate* is a position created for the purpose of this book. There are three very distinct things happening in your life after a death—the raw upheaval of your grief, your desire to prepare a memorable send-off for your loved one, and the logistics of laying your loved one to rest. The first two are emotional, and the third is financial. The powerful emotions of death can completely eclipse the overwhelming expense of the funeral until it is too late. Since funerals and burials can range from $8,000-$20,000 or more, the financial aspect can have long-term consequences for your family. Therefore, I recommend using a family member or friend to become your *Advocate* to attend to the business side of your funeral. This person should be less emotionally impacted by the death than the person who has suffered the greatest loss. The *Advocate*'s purpose is to gather information and pricing for the bereaved and present options to help them make decisions.

So, whether your answer is burial or cremation, once you have made your decision, it is time to gather *General Price Lists* and compare the pricing of local funeral homes and cemeteries if you hope to save money. The *Advocate* would be the person charged with this task. The importance of this step will be reinforced over and over in the subsequent chapters of this book. Meanwhile, here are your options for laying your loved one to rest:

Burial

Many people are uncomfortable with cremation and may make it clear to their families before death that they want to be buried. Sometimes, the family prefers burial because visiting their loved one's gravesite in a cemetery is comforting. However, many families also choose to bury their loved one's ashes in a grave or a columbarium for the same reason. Choosing burial may imply that there will be a formal funeral service with or without a viewing at the funeral home or in a church, but there are also other options, including *Immediate Burial*, which is discussed below.

If you choose a traditional funeral with burial, funeral directors are prepared to move and embalm the body and move forward with a funeral in three to five days. However, there is no rush; your family, not the funeral director, should determine the timing. It is your right to:

- compare pricing among local funeral homes before selecting one.
- investigate the costs of funeral goods, especially caskets, at the funeral home and online.
- take the time needed to gather your family.
- take time to plan, organize, and personalize your service.

You may not be aware that the Federal Trade Commission requires every funeral home in the U.S. to offer a bare-bones price for a *Direct Cremation* or *Immediate Burial*. These options offer only the basic services of cremating or burying your loved one. There is no visitation, no funeral, and no service at the cemetery, but choosing one of these options can significantly reduce the price of your loved one's final expenses. If you never see a *General Price List* (GPL), you will not know these less expensive options are available. Without understanding your rights, you might be swept up into a cremation or funeral package that includes a visitation and all of the features of a full-service funeral, including the price. It also might include items you do not need or may choose not to use. See *Chapter 14* for more details.

Immediate Burial

Some people are unaware of this option, but you will find it on the *General Price List* of every funeral home. It refers to burying your loved one soon after death and before a funeral/memorial service. People choose this method of interment for a variety of reasons. Some are uncomfortable with cremation so an *Immediate Burial* may be a lower-cost option than a full-service funeral. Others may prefer *Immediate Burial* so they can delay a memorial service or celebration of life to a later time or different location in the same way they might after a cremation.

In this scenario, your loved one is picked up from the place of death by the funeral director and held for burial. You can choose a simple casket or even a burial shroud, and whether or not you use the funeral home after burial to plan your service is your choice.

This option utilizes the funeral director to:

- purchase a low-cost casket or take delivery of a casket you purchase online.
- transport the deceased from the place of death.
- store the body.
- provide paperwork for the death certificate.
- secure necessary permits for transportation and burial.
- coordinate the burial with the cemetery.
- transport the body to the cemetery.

At the cemetery, you must:

- purchase a cemetery plot.
- purchase a grave liner unless you have chosen a green cemetery.
- pay for the opening and closing of the grave.
- purchase a headstone or marker at a later time if you choose.

However, if you choose *Immediate Burial*, it is likely that *you will not be informed when the interment occurs* since it will be scheduled at the convenience of the funeral director and the cemetery. You may incur an additional cost if you wish to be present for the burial. The FTC requires that every funeral home in the U.S. offer this service, so if you don't see this on the *General Price List*, ask about it. This should be the lowest-cost burial option, and the fine print should indicate that the *Basic Services Fee* is included in the cost. Be sure you get a detailed invoice before you agree to this option.

Immediate Burial saves money by eliminating:

- preparation of the body, which includes cosmetic enhancements and embalming.
- fees to use the funeral home for a visitation or staff to plan a visitation or a funeral.
- the need for a costly casket. A simple pine box or a shroud is sufficient.
- transportation costs

Important note: This option does not mean you can't have a funeral. After the burial, you can prepare a service that is the same as a funeral in every way except that it is now called a *memorial service* or celebration of life. It can be held at any venue of your choice: a church, restaurant, home, community hall, or park. Using the CHECKLIST in *Chapter* 5, you have all the steps needed to organize a celebration yourself without paying the funeral director to do it for you, and you can take your time.

There is some confusion between an Immediate Burial and a Green Burial. They are not the same. Please see the end of this chapter for detailed information on Green Burials to compare them to the information above regarding Immediate Burials.

Cremation

Cremations have been steadily rising in the U.S. due to their perceived lower cost. However, before choosing this option, it is important to secure a *General Price List* from the funeral home and read *Chapter* 14 to help you understand cremation pricing. Additionally, by choosing cremation, cemetery costs can be reduced, delayed, or eliminated.

Beware of this erroneous assumption regarding cremation

Before moving forward, let's discuss a common misconception regarding cremation. Most families believe that cremation is a less costly choice, but it is not as straightforward as you may think.

As families began to choose cremation over burial to save money, funeral homes began to find ways to make up lost revenue. They created "cremation packages" with critical items missing, like a cremation container or the fee for the crematorium. You need these items, but if you do not see a

General Price List and read the fine print, you will not discover the missing items until you receive the final invoice. The final price will likely be higher than the initial package price you were quoted. By then, it is too late. Your bill may be increased by $300 to $1,000 or more and covered by a disclaimer on the GPL. At that point, you have no recourse. All you can do is pay the bill.

In 2006, the cremation rate in the U.S. was 33.8%; by 2011, it had risen to 42%; and in 2021, families chose cremation 57.5% of the time. Projections indicate that by 2040, the number of cremations is expected to rise to at least 78%. If you have decided to cremate your loved one, you have a few choices:

> Option 1—Visit one to three funeral homes, obtain a copy of their *General Price List*, and study pricing for *Direct Cremation*.
>
> Option 2—Visit a direct cremation facility and obtain their *General Price List*—no further analysis needed.

If you choose option 1, use **Funeral Home Price Comparison Worksheet** in *Appendix B* to see what each price list includes or omits. Compare funeral home costs to those of a direct cremation facility. Be sure the funeral home includes the cost of the cremation container and the cost of a third-party crematory in its pricing. Eliminating key items often makes the funeral home's pricing appear competitive with that of a direct cremation facility when it is not. See *Chapter 14* for detailed pricing information and comparisons regarding cremation options.

Cremation with a funeral using a funeral home

This choice is for families who choose to have a funeral or memorial service, either with or without cremains being present. After death, your loved one will be moved from the place of death to the funeral home. You may be called to positively identify your loved one and sign a release form stating that you want to proceed with cremation.

Note that the FTC's Funeral Rule states that the body does not have to be embalmed if there is no viewing, nor do you have to purchase an expensive casket for cremation. However, you will be required to purchase a simple cremation container made of wood, fiberboard, or cardboard to transfer the body to the crematorium. https://www.ftc.gov/business-guidance/resources/complying-funeral-rule#the-general-price-list

> ***The cremation container should cost no more than $300. Before signing a contract with a funeral home, be sure you know its cost and whether or not it is included in the stated price.***

Many smaller funeral homes do not have crematoriums and must schedule the cremation around other funeral homes in the area. After the body is cremated, the cremains will be returned to you in an inexpensive cardboard or plastic container unless stated otherwise. Families often purchase an urn from the funeral home or online for an upcoming funeral, memorial service, storage at home, or burial of the cremains. If families choose to have the cremains or a body present before the cremation, the service is called a *funeral*. It is called a *memorial service* if they decide to have a service without the cremains or a body present.

Direct Cremation through a funeral home

When you choose the *Direct Cremation* option, you have decided that the funeral home will provide only the basic services needed for cremation, and there will not be a visitation or a funeral at the time of death. The funeral director moves the body from the place of death to a funeral home. The family may be given 15–30 minutes to say goodbye, identify their loved one, and sign an authorization for cremation. The funeral director at the facility will provide the necessary permits and prepare the death certificate. The funeral home will store the body until cremation can be arranged. Some families choose this option to reduce costs or if they decide not to have a funeral or a memorial service at the time of death.

The FTC says: "*Under the Funeral Rule, funeral directors who offer Direct Cremations may not tell you that state or local law requires a casket because none do; must disclose in writing your right to buy an unfinished wood box or an alternative container for a direct cremation; and must make an unfinished wood box or other alternative container available for direct cremations.*"
https://consumer.ftc.gov/articles/choosing-funeral-provider

Cremation at a direct cremation facility

You can arrange cremation with a national organization or find an independent crematory in your vicinity. If you contract with a direct cremation facility, they will pick up your loved one from the place of death, take them directly to their crematorium, and arrange a short visitation for your family to say your goodbyes. At this time, you will positively identify your loved one and formally authorize the cremation. Once completed, they will return the ashes to your family in a basic container.

Facilities that offer these packages employ licensed funeral directors, who will also file the information for the death certificate and may only provide you with one copy. The cost of the funeral director, transportation costs, cremation, and the cremation container are included in your pricing. You can make your decision in advance or at the time of death. My inquiries indicated that the price for pre-planning and pre-paying for cremation may be 20% less expensive than contracting for services at the time of death.

Interment after cremation

Some families may keep their loved one's ashes, while others may scatter them. For these families, there will be no cemetery costs. However, other families may choose burial or interment of the cremains, including purchasing a plot, niche, or columbarium at a cemetery. These options incur cemetery fees, and each of these options should be itemized on the cemetery's price list. Be sure to check all your prices carefully before you agree to the final invoice.

If the deceased is to be interred after cremation, the cemetery may or may not require you to purchase a vault that preserves the cremated remains' integrity and the gravesite's stability. Placing a biodegradable container directly into the earth may break down over time and cause the remains to become indistinguishable from the earth. This is only a problem if your family decides to relocate your loved one's cremains at a later time.

A hybrid of two decisions—a more expensive choice

Some families want a traditional funeral with a viewing but also choose to have their loved one cremated after the funeral. In this case, a casket can be rented for the visitation and funeral, incurring an additional cost of up to a thousand dollars. Due to a time delay, the funeral home may require that the body be embalmed, especially if there is to be a visitation. Cremation occurs after the funeral service.

Does religion affect the decision to cremate or bury?

Sometimes, a person's religious beliefs may determine how they decide between burial and cremation. It is important that family members honor the religious beliefs and traditions of their deceased family members.

Religions and the practice of cremation:

- Hinduism is the only religion that mandates cremation.
- Buddhism has a variety of burial practices, and both cremation and burial are common.
- Most Protestant denominations are neutral on cremation, leaving it up to the individual, nor do they dictate what can be done with cremains. Ashes can be kept by the family, scattered, or buried. In all cases, these faiths believe that the body should be treated with respect until it is interred.
- Lutherans do not object to cremation but prefer that either the cremains or the body be present at the funeral.
- The Methodist Church believes that burial or cremation is a matter of personal choice.
- Presbyterians believe that a body may be buried, cremated, or donated to science.
- Catholicism has permitted cremation since 1963, but the cremains must be buried or entombed in a columbarium at a cemetery. The Catholic belief is that the cremains should be treated the same way as a deceased body; therefore, ashes may not be scattered or kept at home but rather should be interred in a cemetery.
- Episcopalians have a theology similar to Catholicism.
- The Church of Latter-Day Saints does not prohibit cremation, but the practice is discouraged.

Some religions forbid or discourage cremation:

- Islam has one of the strictest prohibitions against cremation; in fact, the body must be buried soon after death.

- The Eastern Orthodox Church does not permit cremation.
- Traditional Jewish law is clear that the deceased must be buried in the earth, but Reform Judaism is modifying the practice since the Talmud does not explicitly forbid cremation.

Decide on a final resting place for your loved one

Will it be a cemetery or mausoleum in the city or town of birth or death? Will the body or the cremated remains be moved to another location? Will ashes be scattered? This subject is covered in detail in *Chapter 4*.

Donating your body to science

Few people consider this for themselves or a loved one at the moment of death, but there are altruistic and financial reasons you might have this discussion beforehand. Donating your body to science may result in consequential scientific research. All medical schools and many research facilities need body donations, which are used for training or research for one to three years, then cremated, sometimes at no cost to you, and the ashes are returned to your family for final interment in your chosen manner.

Donating to a medical school may train several doctors in anatomy, physiology, and surgical techniques. If you choose donation, contact a hospital or a medical school near you. Your loved one can pre-register before death, or your family can donate at the time of death. Financially, the donation may mean that your family has no final expenses unless you use a cemetery for interring the cremains, and you will have a year or more to prepare for this expense. If body donation is a consideration for your family, contact the medical school or research facility that you are considering for more information.

A word of caution: Be sure to register at a carefully vetted university or medical school. A disturbing trend has come to my attention: Some disreputable funeral homes or crematoriums may be dealing with "body brokers." If this issue concerns you, consider reading the article listed below.
https://www.reuters.com/investigates/special-report/usa-bodies-brokers/

Body donation and your funeral service

You may wonder how donating your loved one's body to science might impact your funeral service since your loved one will be absent. The answer is simple. A funeral and a memorial service are the same in layout and design. The only difference is that a funeral has a body or cremains present, and a memorial service does not. It is just terminology. Proceeding with a memorial service shortly after death is perfectly acceptable, but you can also wait until your loved one's cremains are returned to your family, and then you will have a funeral. One of my family members donated her body to a medical school. She had died near her son, six hundred miles from her hometown. Her family had a funeral in her hometown a year later after her cremains were returned. Note: *There are some reasons a body might be disqualified for donation, including obesity,* HIV, *or other contagious diseases, including* COVID-19.

Organ or tissue donation

If your loss is tragic, the last thing that you might want to consider at the time of death is organ or tissue donation. However, knowing that a part of your loved one can live on in another is powerful for some people. The hospital or EMTs can assist you in making this possible if you are willing to consider this option. However, organ donation is time-sensitive for the organs to remain viable. Many states indicate the donor's wishes on a driver's license. In this case, it has been pre-determined by the deceased before a crisis making the decision easy. But even if your loved one has not considered donation, you can still make the decision at the time of death.

What is a Green Burial?

This is sometimes called a *natural burial* and may be confused with a Direct Burial. "A *green burial* is the interment of a deceased person in the soil in a manner that does not inhibit decomposition.

According to the Green Burial Council, a green burial is a way of caring for the dead with minimal environmental impact that aids in the conservation of natural resources, reduction of carbon emissions, protection of worker health, and the restoration and/or preservation of habitat." This manner of disposition rejects using any material that is not biodegradable, such as caskets, grave liners, or burial vaults, as well as harmful chemicals, such as traditional embalming fluid. https://www.greenburialcouncil.org/.

According to www.everloved.com, traditional burials use the equivalent of four million acres of forests for caskets annually and 800,000 gallons of formaldehyde, a toxic chemical that can then get absorbed into the earth, air, and water, plus the burial of huge quantities of metal each year. Even one cremation can release 535 pounds of CO2 and other pollutants into the environment, the equivalent of a 609-mile car trip. www.earthfuneral.com

To maintain a national standard, the *Green Burial Council* has established criteria for approved products and the certification of funeral homes and cemeteries that offer green burials. These include:

- Embalming fluids that are approved by the *Green Burial Council.*
- Use of a container or shroud made only of natural, biodegradable materials without a concrete or metal vault.
- Use of an approved cemetery that restricts memorial markers to preserve natural views that focus on cultivating native plants.

Does every state have green funeral homes and cemeteries?

Only thirty-seven states currently have these facilities, including two hundred and three funeral homes and sixty-one cemeteries certified by the *Green Burial Council* standards.

Where can I find a certified green burial funeral home and cemetery?

The website www.everloved.com has compiled a list of green funeral homes and cemeteries by state. For more specific information on each cemetery, see https://www.greenburialcouncil.org/cemeteries.html.

How can a cemetery become certified to provide green burials?

The *Green Burial Council* has created a certification process for providers to indicate that they wish to comply with the standards of the council. This certification process ensures uniformity among all providers based on the science of human decomposition and the environment. https://www.greenburialcouncil.org/green_burial_defined.html

Cemeteries have three options to comply according to the *Green Burial Council*:

- Hybrid cemetery
- Natural burial grounds
- Conservation burial grounds

See this link for a complete chart of the differences in criteria. https://www.greenburialcouncil.org/our_standards.html

The challenges of a green burial

In 2006, there was only one green burial cemetery in the U.S. Even though there are many more now, finding a green funeral home or cemetery near you may still be challenging. You are dealing with a deceased body rather than cremains, and it will be up to you to arrange transportation by a registered provider to a certified location, possibly hundreds of miles away, which can be costly. *Chapter* 12

Want more details? Check out the Green Burial Council website for everything you need to know about the burial process and its science. https://www.greenburialcouncil.org/green_burial_defined.html.

To learn more about green burial or advocate for the practice, see the following link: https://www.greenburialcouncil.org/recommended_reading.html

Green cremation — water cremation — bio cremation

Alkaline hydrolysis is considered an alternative to flame cremation. It is a combination of water and potassium hydroxide, which is heated to 320 degrees F. Pressure in the container keeps the water from boiling. This initiates a reaction that speeds up the decomposition of the body's soft tissues, which leaves behind only bone fragments and a sterile liquid. When the process is complete, white, soft, porous bone remains, which can be crushed in the hand. The bone fragments are the cremains that are returned to the family.

The process takes only four to six hours, or as long as eighteen hours if a lower temperature is used. Water cremation is considered a green process because it uses one-quarter of the energy of flame-based cremation while producing less carbon dioxide and pollutants. As of 2022, alkaline hydrolysis is legal in twenty-four states, and some medical schools and universities use this process to dispose of unclaimed donor bodies. The cost can be $2,000–$3,000 rather than $1,000 for fire cremation.

However, it should be noted that the Roman Catholic Church in the U.S. does not approve of liquid cremation because the solution that remains after the process, which is the by-product of dissolving all soft tissues in the body, is disposed of into the sewer system. The Church considers it disrespectful to the sanctity of the human body. https://en.wikipedia.org/wiki/Water_cremation#

Summary

Once you decide how to lay your loved one to rest, you can proceed with your plans to honor them. To plan a funeral or memorial service, make arrangements with your house of worship, funeral home, or an independent facility. You may choose to secure a time and date with a venue for a celebration of life. You can even plan a less formal service at a park or in another state, now or in the future. These decisions are the personal choice of each family, guided by their culture, faith, and family traditions. Gathering your family and remembering your loved one may be more important than how you lay your loved one to rest. The first is for the living, and the second is for the deceased. It is the living who feel the loss and need to grieve, and gathering with family surrounds them with love and comfort to help them start moving through the grieving process.

Remember, the first decision you must make after death is not which funeral home you would like to use but whether you will cremate or bury your loved one.

Chapter 3

Choosing a Funeral Home and the Role of the Funeral Director

- *As stated in the previous chapter, it is important that you do not choose a funeral home until you have made the decision to bury or cremate your loved one.*
- *Hopefully, your loved one has made their wishes known before death.*
- *Shopping for a funeral home is difficult at this time, but it is the only way to maintain control of your funeral costs.*
- *Ask a relative or friend to become your Advocate and visit two or three funeral homes in your area to get copies of their General Price Lists before you make your choice.*

The idea of shopping for a funeral home may feel absurd, and this may be the first time you have ever considered it. Naturally, you assume that if you experience a death, you will use the funeral home that your family has always used or the one closest to you. However, this is a decades-old notion that has outgrown its time. It belongs to the same era when no one locked their doors at night.

> ***Somewhere between the advent of the internet and accessing it on your wrist, the entire funeral industry changed, but because our culture does not want to think or talk about death, no one noticed.***

The concept of visiting multiple funeral homes before choosing one maintains that you should compare the prices of all of the funeral homes in your locale before choosing one. Since most people don't want to think about death before they experience it, they assume that all funeral businesses are the same, but they are not. Funeral homes can be as different as restaurants in price, quality, and service. Some are privately owned, and some are owned by large funeral corporations. Pricing for comparable funeral goods and services in the same locale can vary by thousands of dollars, as will be illustrated in *Chapter* 14 of this book.

The funeral home

In past decades, the funeral home in every community was owned by a neighbor. There was a fiduciary relationship built on respect and compassion. The funeral director made a living by burying their community's neighbors and friends. He had a monopoly in the funeral business because no one else wanted the job.

The FTC says: "*There's a trend toward consolidation in the funeral home industry, and many neighborhood funeral homes may appear to be locally owned when, in fact, they're owned by a national corporation. If this issue is important to you, you may want to ask if the funeral home is independent and locally owned.*"
https://consumer.ftc.gov/articles/choosing-funeral-provider

However, in the past twenty-five years, large funeral corporations have purchased many local funeral homes while retaining the business's original family name and sometimes even re-employing the family. Now, rather than answering to their neighbors, they answer to corporate shareholders. The result has been a dramatic rise in the cost of funerals. In some areas, their business model has been so successful that it has been adopted by privately owned funeral homes that serve as competitors within the same area.

The funeral director

You may have never thought about the role of a funeral director before, but by the nature of their profession, they are involved in all deaths in a community. Funeral directors are trained, licensed, and state-certified persons who handle the deceased either for embalming and burial or cremation. They have a legal mandate from their state to maintain the chain of custody of a body from the place of death to cremation or interment. It is also the funeral director's role to record the death and report it to the state. If you choose a traditional funeral with burial, you may have to make almost a hundred decisions in the two to seven days following the death, and selecting a funeral home is one of the first decisions you must make.

The way it has always been

When the funeral director picks up your loved one from the place of death and transports them to their funeral home, it implies that their business will perform all the services you need until the body is interred, including planning the funeral. It has always been assumed that they will provide goods like caskets, urns, grave liners, etc., required to prepare your loved one's funeral.

> ***Funeral directors have a legal mandate from their state to maintain the chain of custody of a body from the place of death to cremation or interment.***

The cost of funerals

By now, you may see where this is leading. The cost of a funeral is one of the four most expensive purchases you will make in your lifetime after your home, car, and the cost of a college education. Let me pose this question. If your loved one had not just passed, would you make any other $8,000–

$30,000 purchase without considering your other options or comparing prices? Of course, you wouldn't. While price-shopping at this time feels like madness and impossible for you, someone in your family— an in-law or a friend acting as your *Advocate*—might be willing to do it for you.

> ***Let's return to the question posed at the beginning of this book: "How much money do you need in your bank account so that a $20,000 expense in the next week is not considered a significant withdrawal?***

By now, you may be asking, "Is there any way I can lower the cost of a funeral?" A cautious answer is "yes," but only if you are willing to do some work, and I confess that it is exponentially easier if you are willing to do the work *before* you experience a death.

Judy's story

A friend lost her mother. Without researching funeral homes, she visited the funeral home in her neighborhood. After discussing prices with the funeral director, she was shocked to learn the cost. Her father had passed away a few years before, and she remembered the price of the funeral being significantly less than she had just been quoted. After discussing this with her siblings, she decided to obtain prices from the funeral home that the family had used for her dad. She was stunned to learn that the price would be 50% lower than the first funeral home she had contacted. Her mother's estate had enough money to cover the cost of the funeral at the first funeral home, but the money saved by using the second funeral home could become part of the children's inheritance. This was not a difficult decision, but it illustrates how significantly prices may vary for the same services in the same region, and all it took was a second phone call. These funeral homes were in a suburb of a major city in the Northeast.

> ***Basically, the choice was to use her mother's money to pay the funeral home or provide an inheritance for her siblings. What do you think her mother would have wanted?***

This was not a difficult decision for her, but it illustrates how significantly prices may vary for the same services in the same region, and all it took was a second phone call. These funeral homes were in a suburb of a major city in the Northeast.

What do you want your funeral service to look like?

Take a moment to ask yourself what you want regarding a funeral service. Be honest with yourself, and then be honest with your family. It will be helpful to ask these questions now. If you choose the full-service concierge funeral, it will be beautiful. Still, it will cost $15,000 or more, NOT including a cemetery plot, opening and closing the grave, and the cost of a grave liner, marker, or other cemetery charges, which could be an additional $8,000–$20,000 or more.

Here's what you can do to buy time while you shop around

Determine if there are any costs associated with a delay in not choosing a funeral home immediately. Tell the person asking you which funeral home you would like to use that you need more time to investigate your options. Ask them how long you can delay. Inform them that the cost of the funeral is a serious consideration for you and that you would like to investigate an Immediate Burial or a Direct Cremation for your loved one. Or tell them you would like to compare a few funeral homes before deciding so you can evaluate costs and services and check reviews. Note that you should expect the hospital or morgue holding your loved one to charge $50–$100 or more per day for the delay. This may not be possible if your loved one is in an elder care facility, since the fine print of your contract may state that the room needs to be cleared within a few hours. However, suppose a funeral director transports your loved one to their funeral home, and after researching, you decide to use another facility. One of two things could happen:

- First, you have only a matter of hours to make the uncomfortable decision to move to a second funeral home. Moving your loved one from Funeral Home A to B could cost you hundreds if not over a thousand dollars in transportation costs, but if the cost of a funeral at Funeral Home A is $15,000 and the cost at Funeral Home B, it is only $8,000 a move might be prudent.

- Second, if you hesitate too long, Funeral Home A may begin basic preparations of the body, and the *Basic Services Fee* for that funeral home will go into effect, costing you $1,800–$5,700. At that point, a move may not be practical.

Clearly, these situations illustrate that it would be best to have made your decision before you experienced a death or, at the very least, before you choose a funeral home if the death has already occurred. The time between losing a loved one and choosing a funeral home could be one to three hours. This is very little time in anyone's world, but it feels like a blink of an eye in your mental state. But if you do not take control of the funeral process at this time, you may surrender your rights and bank account to the funeral home you choose.

The FTC says: "*Comparison shopping doesn't have to be difficult, especially if it's done before the need for a funeral arises. Thinking ahead can help you make informed and thoughtful decisions about funeral arrangements. It allows you to choose the specific items you want and need and to compare the prices several funeral providers charge.*" https://consumer.ftc.gov/articles/choosing-funeral-provider

Shopping for funeral homes—really?

The subtitle indicates that this book will not only help you navigate the logistics of laying your loved one to rest but also give you tools to help you control costs. So, whether your answer is burial or cremation, once you have made your decision—as crazy as it sounds—it is time to shop for funeral services. You can do this by gathering *General Price Lists* and comparing the pricing of local funeral homes and cemeteries in your area. This is your only hope of saving money at the time of death. The importance of this step will be reinforced repeatedly in the subsequent chapters of this book.

As you read the above paragraph, I am sure you think I have stepped over the line of reality, but please don't check out just yet. I assure you that shopping for a funeral home absolutely *can* and *must* be done, and this book will give you the tools to accomplish it. You don't have to figure it out for yourself. I have done it several times, but *you* have to do the legwork.

Gather price lists

Gathering price lists is easier than you think! The FTC has given you the right to go into any funeral home in the U.S. and request a *General Price List* (GPL) without giving your name or sitting for a conference. My experience is that you can be in and out of most funeral homes in less than five minutes with their GPL in hand. Unfortunately, if it takes more than five minutes, the cost of a funeral at that funeral home may be much higher than the competition. Don't take my word for it; do your own research and visit all the funeral homes in your immediate area to see if my theory holds up. Make it a game long before you have a need, and share what you learn with your neighbors, relatives, and friends. They will all thank you.

> **Your Script: It's this simple!**
>
> ***"Could I please get a copy of your price list? Does this price list include the price of caskets and burial containers?" If the answer is no: "Could I please get a copy of those prices, too?" You might want to add: "Are you a family-owned funeral home?"***

In my experience, there seem to be two kinds of funeral homes, those that focus on service and those that focus on sales. Which would you rather do business with? You'll never know which is which until you walk into their business to get a copy of their GPL. Once inside, you will either feel comfortable as they give you the price lists without question or uncomfortable if they try to escort you to a room, make you wait, and begin the sales pressure as they try to obtain your personal information and attempt to start a sales consultation—all the while confusing you to the point that you forget what you went in for—that all-important *General Price List.*

> ***You can determine the funeral home's business model within five minutes of visiting their facility. It's definitely worth your time.***

Shopping for pre-need funeral services

A note of caution: If you decide to shop for end-of-life or pre-need funeral services before death, you should shop all of the funeral homes in your area and obtain *General Price Lists.*

The best approach is NOT to inform them of what you are doing. Enter each business, request a *General Price List*, refuse to give your name if asked or have an alias ready, and return to your car immediately. Once you allow a conversation to begin, in many cases, so will the sales pressure. The **Funeral Home Price Comparison Worksheet** in *Appendix* B has all the tools you need to decide the best fit for your family and budget. After comparing the funeral homes in your area, then and only then should you sit for a pre-need conference.

Meanwhile, here is a real-life example of how you can be financially sabotaged during the fog of grief. An acquaintance lost her husband. I asked her, "What was your experience with the funeral home when your husband passed away?" It was an innocent question, one to which I honestly expected a one-sentence or even a one-word answer. Imagine my shock as she revealed her experience.

Rosa's story

"The experience was awful," she exclaimed. Norm had been sick and in assisted living for some time. Near the end, Rosa moved him to a hospice facility. Meanwhile, knowing time was short with her beloved husband, Rosa purchased a pre-paid funeral plan from her neighborhood's ABC family-owned funeral home.

At the time of Norm's passing, the hospice facility said they would take care of getting Norm transported to the funeral home. Rosa indicated she had made arrangements at the ABC funeral home in her neighborhood. They acknowledged her, and she thanked them and went home for the night. In the morning, Rosa went to the ABC funeral home to begin planning the funeral. ABC was shocked that Norm had passed and said they were sorry but did not have Norm's body. Consider her panic and confusion. "Where is he?" she exclaimed. We're sorry, Rosa, but we've had no contact from the hospice facility.

Imagine the thoughts swirling in her head. Grief from just losing her husband eight hours earlier, shock that she did not know the location of his body, confusion and anger about how this could have happened when she had been so clear with the hospice facility, and helplessness at where to begin looking for him in a city of several million people.

Fortunately, Rosa had a son who was a police detective to help her unravel this mystery, and several hours later, after numerous phone calls, she found Norm at the upscale XYZ funeral home 15 miles from her residence in the heart of the city. Rosa could not let this happen. She now had three problems. First, she could not lose the money she had pre-paid to the ABC funeral home. Second, she did not want to use—nor could she afford—the upscale XYZ funeral home. Third, her only choice was to pay for ABC to pick up Norm's body from XYZ and transfer him to their facility. In the end, Rosa was billed for the first transfer from the hospice facility to XYZ and now had to pay for Norm to be transported to the ABC funeral home. It should be noted that the average cost of transporting a body in her city is $1,100.

Do you think this was an accident or a financial arrangement between the hospice facility or one of its employees and the XYZ funeral home? Neither Rosa nor I know the answer, but at this point, she had spent approximately $2,200 before beginning to plan Norm's funeral.

Just a thought

When things like this happen, survivors often suffer silently out of respect for their deceased loved one. Complaining about money after a death would be perceived as disrespectful to their loved one. Months later, they may quietly admit to a close friend that they might have made different choices had they been able to think clearly. This notion is only partially true. The only way to make clearer choices is to make them beforehand so you don't have to make them at a debilitating time like this.

> ***The universal silence of most of its customers allows bad actors in the funeral industry to continue their business model unchallenged. Resolve to speak out to your family and friends if you feel you have been unfairly treated or unjustly charged. This is not a reflection on you but on the industry that took advantage of you in your hour of grief.***

Summary

After a death, the moment you choose a funeral home is one of the most vulnerable times of your life. There are three things at play:

- First, your mind is reeling, and your emotions are out of control, especially if the death was tragic or unexpected, and your ability to make even simple decisions is paralyzed.
- Second, as you begin the planning process, your only thought is to silently scream, "I just want this to be over!" Followed by, "I can't make any decisions now!" but you are forced to make them anyway. So, it's easy to let the funeral director take over. The thought of cost may occur to you in the back of your mind, but you do not have the bandwidth to process any of that right now.
- Third, you must quickly choose a funeral home to care for your loved one until they are laid to rest. Unfortunately, your choices are limited to a few funeral homes in your area, and time is short.

It is important to remember that the funeral industry is a business. They have expenses and a right to make a living, but you have rights, too. You have the right to clear and transparent pricing and the right to have a dignified send-off for your loved one at a reasonable price. You also have the right to lay your loved one to rest without being upsold frivolous or over-priced goods, and you absolutely can't do it without actively participating in the process. *Blindly trusting the funeral director and hoping for the best is a $15,000–$25,000 expense waiting to happen.*

> ***I want to pause to say that most funeral homes are upstanding businesses run with integrity. Most funeral directors are compassionate people who genuinely want to help you in your hour of need. Still, across the board, prices for their services are substantial.***

As I began collecting and analyzing pricelists from around the country, I was shocked to learn of the thousands of dollars charged in *hidden* or, shall I say, *less-than-transparent fees.* My experience is that the more pages you find in the GPL and the smaller the fine print, the more you will pay for your funeral, but don't take my word for it. Visit at least two funeral homes in your area.

The moment you choose a funeral home, you are at their mercy. Your emotions, time cost, and a lack of understanding of the funeral industry are all your enemies now. This is why I suggest gathering information in advance and securing an *Advocate* to become your business manager if you have recently suffered a death. *But the best plan is to read this book long before you need it so you can do some research before you experience the stress of losing a loved one.*

I am the quiet voice of your future, saying that not taking the time to research funeral homes in your area or thinking about the goods or services you want before you need them may be a very costly mistake.

The problem you face at the moment of death is that you do not have the option to refuse to purchase these services. Your need is immediate, and the timeline is short. Remember, these choices could affect your family's finances for years as you continue to pay for goods and services that you will scarcely remember one year from the day of the funeral.

Notes

Chapter 4

The Interment: To Bury, Entomb, or Scatter

- *Burial, committal, and interment are words used interchangeably to describe a deceased person's return to the earth and can refer either to a body or cremated remains.*
- *The decision to bury or cremate determines families' choices for interment.*
- *This chapter gives you options in each category so you can get an overview before making a final choice.*

Choosing a cemetery

If your loved one is to be interred, it is time to choose a cemetery. Selecting the burial place may be determined by factors unique to each family. The cemetery should be contacted early in the funeral planning process, usually within twenty-four to thirty-six hours after death, to ensure the burial flows with your funeral service.

> **The FTC warns:** "*In the short time between the death and burial of a loved one, many family members find themselves rushing to buy a cemetery plot or grave—often without careful thought or a personal visit to the site. That's why it's in the family's best interest to buy cemetery plots before you need them.*"
>
> https://consumer.ftc.gov/articles/choosing-funeral-provider

---

If you are the first in your family to experience a death, and your loved one has expressed a desire to be buried, you might find yourself rushing to find a burial plot. The next question will be, do you want one plot for the deceased or several plots for future deaths in your family? Most funeral directors partner with local cemeteries and can assist you in making burial arrangements. However, working directly with a cemetery is also an option.

NOTE: A burial plot is a 4' x 8' burial space, while a burial lot is one or more contiguous spaces. These lots contain two or four graves. If you are the first person in your family unit to pass away, your family must decide which to purchase. The purchase of a lot can substantially add to your final burial cost but ask the cemetery if the additional graves can be paid for over time.

Individual plots generally range between $1,500 and $5,000, but prices vary based on region, state, and whether you live in a rural or urban area. For example, the cost of a grave site in the rural area I have chosen for burial is only $500, but this can rise to $20,000 or more in larger urban areas where land costs are high, and cemeteries are filling up.

In smaller towns or rural areas, it is typical for each church or denomination to have its own cemetery. Cemeteries may be established in cities for veterans or various religions or ethnicities. You may also find cemeteries owned by municipalities or funeral corporations. Your parents may have purchased a family lot, allowing numerous family members to be buried together. Check out this option for single adults. Also, I have heard of families owning plots in several different states. Note that large urban cemeteries seem to only allow the burial of three urns per plot, but in the rural cemetery I visited, I was told that a single burial plot could bury six cremated family members. If there is no cremation, a burial must occur. To bury your loved one's body, you must choose a casket, grave liner, or burial vault. You must purchase a cemetery plot or find a pre-purchased family lot. You may be considering a monument or marker for future purchase unless one already exists but understand there is no rush to do it now.

The interment will occur immediately after the funeral. You may choose clergy, the funeral director, or a friend to lead the committal service. There may be prayers or inspirational thoughts at the grave site. If your loved one was a veteran, and you have made arrangements in advance, representatives from their branch of service may play "Taps" or present a flag to family members at this time. Before leaving the graveside, family members sometimes shovel the first dirt into the grave and toss flowers onto the casket in one final act of love and respect. In most cases, the family may choose to leave the gravesite if it is too painful to watch the casket as it is lowered into the ground, but it is your choice.

People choose burial over cremation for a variety of reasons. While some religions don't allow cremation, burial may also be a personal choice. Before death, loved ones may express discomfort with cremation. Others want to be buried with a spouse or a child. Sometimes, parents or children find comfort in visiting the grave of a loved one. It is a matter of choice. If you have definite thoughts on the subject, you should clearly communicate your preference to your family while you are living. But it should also be noted that you can only expect your family to honor your wishes for burial if you have prepared financially for this more expensive option.

Opening and closing fees

> ***One unexpected fee that may be charged, even if you have prepaid for burial or pre-purchased your plot, is the fee to open and close the grave, which can be thousands of dollars.***

I learned of a family whose mother had reassured them that she had pre-paid her funeral expenses and purchased her cemetery plot. The children were shocked to learn that they owed almost $4,500 for "opening and closing fees" before burial. The existence of these fees is often misunderstood by clients who assume that when they pay for a cemetery plot, these fees are included in the price, but most likely they are not. I'm sure you will agree that this is a substantial amount of money in anyone's world, but what can you do about it at the time of burial? This fee was likely listed somewhere in the fine print of the purchase agreement. *Another reason to always read the fine print.*

Some cemeteries charge a fee called the *Professional Service Fee* at the cemetery, similar to the *Basic Services Fee* of the funeral home. It may also be called an *Interment Fee*. It covers the cost of meeting with the staff, filing burial permits, excavating the soil, installing the vault, closing the grave, leveling the site, and replacing the sod, among other things. Depending on your location, these fees can range from $200 in a rural area to $5,700 in an urban area. The base fee for your region can dramatically increase if you want your interment to be on a Saturday, Sunday, after-hours, or a holiday.

Entombment in a mausoleum

The most common form of entombment is in a mausoleum, which is usually an above-ground stone building designed for burying numerous caskets in a single space. Mausoleums are popular in cities like New Orleans, where the ground is unfavorable for long-term interment or in cities with dense populations. Mausoleums have a long history, as evidenced by the pyramids in Egypt. They can be managed by a private organization, a religious denomination, or a community and may inter hundreds of individuals in one place. They also can be private for the exclusive use of one family. They may be erected on private property or in a cemetery. For more information, visit the website https://www.usurnsonline.com/.

Additional purchases required for burial—grave liners and burial vaults

Grave liners and burial vaults are also referred to as *burial containers*. Containers are not required by law anywhere in the U.S., but cemetery policies *can and do* require them to keep graves from caving in. Most lawn care is done by heavy mowing equipment; thus, the cemetery usually requires some form of inground burial container to preserve their equipment and maintain an attractive, safe space.

The grave liner covers only the top and sides of the casket but does not encase it, whereas the burial vault may be constructed of concrete, plastic, fiberglass, or metal. The vault is placed in the ground before the family arrives for the burial, and the casket is lowered into the vault. Finally, a cover is placed over the top. A burial vault will be more expensive than a grave liner. Be sure to get a *Burial Container Price List* from the funeral home or the cemetery before you purchase.

A vault may resist water, dirt, and insects, but beware of funeral directors who state that a sealed vault will impede decomposition over time. The opposite may be true, and vaults may be unsealed unbeknownst to you before being placed in the ground. Please do some research if this is a consideration for you.

While visiting a cemetery office, I saw a vault resembling a coffin-sized plastic toolbox. The cost was approximately $500, but the salesperson had to look in several places to find the price. Apparently, the cemetery would have preferred to sell me the $8,500 vault made of hammered metal with gold trim.

> ***The only person who will see the burial container is the person who digs the grave. Neither you nor your family will see it because it will already be in the ground when you arrive for the burial. You will only see a picture at the time of purchase, so I ask—do you really want to spend thousands of dollars on this item?***

Monuments, headstones, and markers

Monuments and headstones are usually made of granite or marble for durability. The headstone includes one or more names – in the case of a husband and wife—and their dates of birth and death. They can be purchased locally or online with free shipping to your location. Local purchases may include installation, but those purchased elsewhere may not. This task has no urgency; it can be done weeks, months, or even years after death. Each cemetery has rules and regulations regarding headstones and grave markers, so check with them before purchasing online. Prices range from $1,500 on the low end to $10,000. The average prices are $3,000–$5,000.

Grave markers

These are plaques that are inlaid into the ground. Many are made of granite or bronze for durability in all weather conditions, but they can also be constructed from marble, sandstone, or slate. The marker will be engraved with the deceased's name, date of birth, and death. They can be made in any size to conform to cemetery regulations. Be sure to check your cemetery's rules before placing your order.

Interment of cremains

If you have chosen cremation, you have several options for cremated remains. Ashes can be buried, placed in a columbarium or mausoleum, scattered from a mountaintop, sent into space, buried at sea, or even turned into a tree. After cremation, remains may be returned to you in a simple cardboard or plastic container. Many families purchase an urn for a funeral service, burial, or to keep at home.

Burial of cremains

The space needed to bury an urn is smaller and, in some cases, less costly to purchase than for the burial of a body. If you choose to bury cremains in a family plot, three to six individuals may be buried in a single 4'x8' plot. Cemetery regulations will vary from rural to urban areas. Most large cemeteries have a special section for burying cremains. These designated areas may have requirements for markers to ensure uniformity. It is also possible to bury the cremains in a family plot. Be advised that the cemetery may require you to purchase a burial vault to encase the urn so it will not be broken during regular cemetery maintenance. Also, the vault allows the cremains to be disinterred and moved to a different location.

The FTC says: "*If you plan to bury your loved one's cremated remains in a mausoleum or columbarium, you can expect to purchase a crypt and pay opening and closing fees, as well as charges for endowment care and other services.*"
https://consumer.ftc.gov/articles/buying-cemetery-site

Private property

Some families choose to bury their loved ones on private property. Check your local ordinances before you do this. Cremated remains are sterile, so there may be fewer constraints. It is recommended that you bury cremains three feet into the earth to reduce the possibility that they will be disturbed. If you think there is a chance that you might move them if you sell the property, choose a stone urn or burial vault for easy relocation.

Scattering ashes

Many families scatter their loved one's ashes in a place significant to the family or the deceased. Ashes may be scattered on uninhabited public lands or waterways. If you need to transport cremains to another location, see *Chapter* 12 for detailed information. Also, some religious faiths require that the cremated remains be placed in the ground, in a mausoleum or columbarium. This is the case if your loved one is buried in the Roman Catholic or Episcopalian faiths. If your family is considering scattering your loved one's ashes, be sure that it agrees with the religious beliefs of your loved one or the faith practice that handles your funeral. *Chapter* 1

Entombment of cremains

An example of the entombment of ashes is a *columbarium*. This appears to be a new trend, but columbaria have been around for thousands of years, dating back to the Roman Empire when cremation was common. Initially, these structures were brick walls with niches for urns and built around an open court. They also were housed in churches in the Old World for hundreds of years. Eventually, they were discontinued and did not return until late in the 20th century.

The trend likely reappeared as cemeteries filled, the cost of land increased, and cremations rose in the U.S. Cemeteries were typically built at the outer edge of a town or city. As urban development has expanded and cemeteries have been surrounded, the revival of columbaria allows for more burials in existing cemeteries.

Today, many cemeteries are constructing granite, marble, or concrete columbaria for cremation urns. These contain several niches for individual urns and become the final resting place for ashes after cremation. Outdoor niches are constructed above ground and are sometimes built into a concrete or granite wall. They can also be free-standing structures or designed as benches or entire buildings.

Columbaria store and display cremated remains. The structure has several compartments, each holding an urn containing the ashes of one individual. The cover of each niche may be marble, granite, or bronze, allowing it to be customized to include information about the deceased, similar to a monument. These niches are available at many cemeteries, some churches, crypts, and crematorium sites. They can accommodate many kinds of urns and several individuals in a relatively small space.

A columbarium can be a permanent or transitional place of remembrance that can accommodate a more mobile lifestyle as families move from place to place. An urn can easily be moved from one cemetery to another to remain with a family as they relocate.

The most common types of niches include:

- Single niches containing a single urn may cost $750–$5,000.
- Double niches for two urns may cost $800–$3000 or add $2,500 to the price of a single niche.
- Family niches with space for four or more urns—check pricing in your location.

A columbarium may also be built indoors with a glass covering that reveals the niche's content. Indoor niches will cost more than outdoor niches since they protect the urn from the elements. Also, niches purchased before death will generally be 20%—25% less expensive than those purchased at the time of death. Note that it is appropriate to inquire about the cleaning and maintenance of the columbaria at the time of purchase.

The size of the niches is generally 9" cubed or 12" cubed for individuals but will be larger if it is to hold more urns. Be sure to ascertain the exact dimensions of the space before ordering your urn. To ensure the security of the cremains, once the niche is sealed, the urn can only be removed by cemetery personnel using special tools.

Summary

This chapter presents multiple options for laying your loved one to rest. Your choice to bury or cremate leads to a complete subset of additional decisions regarding how and where to find a final resting place for yourself or your loved one. Choices may be determined by cost, location, religion, or family preferences. The good news is that there is no right or wrong way to do this.

Since the Federal Trade Commission (FTC) does not regulate cemetery pricing or fees, the cost of burials can vary widely around the country. Pricing in private, rural, or religious-affiliated cemeteries seems to differ vastly from cemeteries in urban areas.

> ***Rapidly rising costs for burial indicate that visiting a cemetery long before you need one is prudent.***

Many people who know they want to be buried choose to purchase their cemetery plots decades before they need them. Also, remember that Episcopalians, Catholics, and possibly other faiths must inter cremated remains in either the ground or a columbarium or mausoleum, so they must use a cemetery. There is some indication that prices can be reduced by as much as 20% by pre-purchasing a plot. You will also likely be able to make payments on your plot or lot, reducing your costs at the time of death. At the very least, visiting a cemetery will inform you of pricing in your area, which could lead you to choose cremation over burial.

One cemetery sales agent told me that two senior clients came in for burial. They each had acquired their plots decades ago, in the 50s, when the original owner purchased a farm and decided to make it a cemetery. One client's family brought in a contract that stated that the purchase price for his plot had been $5.00, and a second had a contract that said his plot price had been a chicken. The cemetery owner had purchased that farm as a gamble, and that chicken may have indicated that he struggled initially. In his nineties and without an heir, he sold his cemetery to a corporation. With thirty acres of land still available for burials in a densely populated region on the east coast, one can only guess how many millions of dollars he made on his gamble.

This chapter emphasizes the difference in price among various forms of interment. It reinforces the idea that shopping for prices at cemeteries is just as vital to your financial well-being as shopping for funeral homes. Remember that cemeteries are not subject to the *Funeral Rule* unless the cemetery and funeral home are owned jointly by a single owner or business; therefore, their fees may be less transparent. This discussion continues in *Chapter 14*.

Rising costs for both funerals and burials, coupled with the declining availability of land in urban areas, ensure that prices will never be lower than they are at the moment you are reading these words. Clearly, the best time to purchase a cemetery plot is today.

Chapter 5

The CHECKLIST Organize Tasks, Delegate, and Plan a Funeral Yourself

- *This* CHECKLIST *informs you of the critical decisions that must be made at the time of death.*
- *It illustrates a top-down approach to the big picture for planning a funeral previously known only to the funeral director.*
- *It unveils the steps involved in planning a funeral by giving you an outline of how to proceed.*
- *Hopefully, this overview prevents you from feeling overwhelmed by the number of decisions you must make in the days and weeks following a death.*

STOP! Remember, you should not choose a funeral home until you decide whether to BURY or CREMATE your loved one. *Chapter 1*

You cannot plan a funeral until this decision is made. If money is a consideration, reread *Chapters* 3 and 4 to understand your options. Also, be sure to investigate cemetery costs before making this decision. Once you choose burial, you incur not only all of the costs and fees of a funeral, but all of the costs and fees related to a burial as well. Combined, they may amount to tens of thousands of dollars, and there are no do-overs once you start down this road. *Chapter 14*

> ***The current business model of some funeral homes is to capture your business at the point of death and to place you on a speeding train. There is no way off once the cars are moving until you finish the ride. By then, you have completed an $8,000–$40,000 purchase. The goods and services have been delivered, and you realize the day after the funeral that "all sales were final!"***

This outline gives you an overview of your options, helping you make informed decisions either before or at the time of death.

☑ **If you choose cremation**

- If cremation is your preference, first decide whether you will use a funeral home or a direct cremation facility for the cremation.
- Deciding to cremate your loved one and postponing a memorial service until later is perfectly acceptable.
- Gather *General Price Lists* from local funeral homes and use the information in *Chapter* 14 to ensure you have the best price for the services you want.
- Do not pay more than $300 for an "alternative cremation container," and be sure that you understand what is included in the Direct Cremation price or other package pricing, as well. *Chapter 14*
- Determine if you will have a service at the time of death or sometime in the future.
- If you decide to have a memorial service at the time of death (without a body or cremains present), follow many of the steps listed below for planning a funeral.
- *Be sure to honor the religious traditions of the deceased regarding cremation.*

☑ **If you choose burial**

- Make a list of the items important to you for the funeral.
- Gather *General Price Lists* from local funeral homes and use the information in *Chapter* 14 to ensure you have the best price for the services you want.
- Understand that you can purchase caskets from another vendor or online without consequences or fees from the funeral home. You can use this information for negotiation.
- Determine if you want to use a church for a visitation, funeral, or a reception.
- If burial is your preference, understand that you can choose Immediate Burial, with a simple wooden casket and no embalming, to give your family the freedom to delay the memorial service.
- If you choose a full-service funeral, know that you can resist being upsold on goods and services.

☑ **What you need to know before choosing a funeral home**

- Read *Chapter* 1 for the detailed reasons of why and how to shop for a funeral home, either at the time of death or beforehand. Also, read *Chapter* 14 to understand industry pricing.
- Be aware of the impact of your grief on your current mental state and how this will cloud your decision-making.
- Financial planners and psychologists tell you not to make major financial decisions for a year or more following a death, yet you will make the third or fourth-largest purchase of your life coupled with dozens of decisions within the next week. Ask for help as you move forward.
- Be sure you understand the "rights" the government has given you with the funeral home under the *Funeral Rule*. *Chapter* 6

☑ **Control the cost of a funeral**

- What is your budget? Most people who are caught off guard by death don't have one.
- Understand that the cost of a funeral and burial can be $20,000 or more unless you are aggressive with your research and decisions from the moment of death.

- Remember, on day one, you can still stop the clock.

> ***Thinking about money at this time is NOT disrespectful to your loved one. In fact, it is important to preserve cash during this time. Remember, you and your children may have to sacrifice for months or even years to pay for these end-of-life services. Keep in mind that the cost of funerals can also seriously diminish potential inheritances. Are you okay with that?***

If you are dealing with a tragic and unexpected death and you don't know how you will pay for these final arrangements, consider the following:

- Get help going against your instinct, and do not mindlessly allow the funeral director to control all funeral arrangements, even if it will simplify your life for a week or two. You will feel they have your best interests at heart, and they do, *in all areas except money*.
- Before choosing a funeral home, obtain *General Price Lists*, *Casket Price Lists*, and *Burial Container Price Lists* from two or three funeral homes.
- Choose a pragmatic friend or relative to be your *Advocate/business manager* and allow them to guide you. Remember, the death of your loved one is a business for the funeral director, and someone must advocate for your financial well-being as well as you move forward.
- If you are lucky enough to have a life insurance policy, do not sign it over to the funeral home. Find a way to pay the invoice and repay yourself or your family from the insurance policy's proceeds. Otherwise, the cost of the funeral will likely equal or even exceed the face value of the policy. Funeral homes are not entitled to know about your insurance or your inheritance.
- Know what you aren't capable of while grieving *(which is most things)*, especially financial decisions.
- Know the least expensive options before you buy anything, especially substantial items like a casket, which may have a markup of as much as 200–700%. Consider purchasing a casket online.
- Decide which services are most important to you, which you can afford, and which you can do without, and then say "no" to everything else.

Keep your future in mind. Ask yourself, "How important will these goods or services be to me one year from today, especially if I am still paying for them?"

- Ask your *Advocate* to help calculate the costs and keep a running tally as you make your choices. Remember, every time you add something, even after you have agreed to the final price, it will increase your final invoice.
- If the process is moving too fast, slow things down to allow you more time to gather information.
- Remember, cremation can save you thousands of dollars over burial and extend your timeline. You can still have a memorial service even if the cremation is pending. This eliminates the urgency of choosing a cemetery and paying those expenses now.
- You may be able to save money by not including the funeral home as a middleman in purchasing flowers, guest books, memorial cards, video presentations, or even a casket. Check out the cost of these items online.
- Beware of "Package" pricing. Be sure it only includes the things you want and everything you need and nothing else. *Chapter 14*

Planning a Funeral

☑ **Gather your family**

- Notify and gather your family and assign tasks from this CHECKLIST to assist with the planning.
- Secure information for the death certificate, including a Social Security card or number. *Chapter 9*
- Begin to go through family photos and choose a flattering headshot of your loved one.
- Identify special mementos, military honors, awards, and religious articles .

☑ **Consider the following difficult choices** *Chapter 2*

- If your loved one's death was sudden, consider organ or tissue donation.

- Did your loved one ever mention donating their body to science? This could reduce the cost of final expenses.

☑ **Decide on a final resting place** *Chapter 4*

- Obtain price lists from two or more cemeteries.
- Visit the cemetery before signing a contract.
- Purchase a plot or columbarium.
- Review cemetery rules.
- Purchase a grave liner or burial vault.
- Be sure you understand all burial costs and fees before you sign a contract.
- Purchase a monument or grave marker (This can be delayed if financially necessary).

☑ **Decide on a funeral, memorial service, or celebration of life** *Chapter 8*

- Will there be a wake/viewing/visitation before the funeral?
- Will you have a religious or secular service?
- Will the service be held at a church, funeral home, or other venue, or will it be postponed to a later time?
- Choose the place and call to secure a date.

☑ **Begin planning your service** *Chapter 8*

◆ **If the service will be at a church**

- Contact and meet with clergy or staff to begin planning the service.
- Choose Scripture.
- Choose music: recorded or live, and secure musicians.
- Determine how your family will be involved in the service: leading, reading, speaking, eulogizing, singing or pallbearers.
- Finalize the order of service and determine who will prepare the funeral program. *Appendix D*

◆ **Funeral home or other venue**

- Begin your outline for the service. *Appendix C*
- Determine who will lead the service: a member of the clergy, a funeral director, or a family member.
- Choose inspirational readings or Scripture.

- Choose music: recorded or live, and secure musicians.
- Determine how the family will be involved in the service, leading, reading, eulogizing, or singing.
- Finalize the order of service.

◆ **General considerations for any service** *Chapter 11*

If the body is not present, will the cremated remains be present?

Will you have:

- A printed order of service, and what will it contain?
- Memorial cards available for guests?
- Envelopes available for donations to a charity or to assist with the funeral costs?
- Flowers? Who will provide them?
- An enlarged, framed photo of your loved one?
- A guestbook? Where will it be placed?
- A memorial video presentation?
- A eulogy? Who will write it? Who will deliver it?

The church or funeral home will determine the placement of these items, including flowers. However, in the case of a celebration at a secular venue, you will need to make these decisions.

☑ **Will you have a reception after the service? Where will it be?** *Chapter 11*

- At a church
- At a restaurant
- At someone's home
- Who will be invited?
- All guests
- Immediate and extended family who may have traveled for the funeral?
- Immediate family only

☑ **Special considerations**

- Who will conduct the graveside service, the funeral director, clergy, or family?
- Who will provide transportation to the funeral or cemetery:
    - a funeral home limousine

- private cars
- a car for flowers

- Will a police escort be necessary for the procession to the cemetery, especially for a large funeral in an urban area?
- Will there be Veteran honors or honors of fraternal organizations at the funeral or the cemetery? Who will make these arrangements?

☑ **Important tasks that family members can oversee** *Chapters 8 & 11*

- Secure photos—old and recent. Make an enlarged photo or two of your loved one.
- Find personal memorabilia—medals, honors, awards.
- Decide how to handle condolence calls and food from friends.
- Plan the eulogy— who will write it, and who will deliver it?
- Write the obituary—Decide where it will be published: in a newspaper, on social media, on a funeral home website, or on another platform.
- Select music and secure musicians; gather sheet music or recordings. Churches will provide most of the music you need if you choose that route.
- Secure copies of sheet music, visit musicnotes.com or sheetmusicplus.com.
- Set up a digital announcement—use the funeral home or your own social media.
- Select Scripture or inspirational readings. *Appendix E*
- Make a decision to accept flowers or choose a charity for your guests to support.
- Decide if you need financial help paying for the funeral or burial—will you use social media or crowdfunding.
- Create a slideshow for use at a wake, funeral, or reception.
- Contact anyone you want to speak at your service—a friend, relative, co-worker, or a member of the family.
- Create or purchase memorial cards.
- Purchase thank you notes.
- Purchase a guest book. Consider the website www.funeralprints.com for covers for your funeral programs, prayer cards, memorial cards, and guest books.

☑ **The death certificate** *Chapter 9*

- Gather the required documents and information as requested by the funeral director, who will order copies from the state.

- Determine how many death certificates you need to settle the estate. You will need one for every financial account you find, plus any other legal entity that must be notified of the death. A good rule to start is 10–15 copies. Life in the coming months will be easier if you order them now.
- Be aware that the funeral director will order the first copies of the death certificate, but all future copies must be ordered from your state, and the funeral director does not keep a copy on file.

☑ **What do you need to do to relocate cremains to or from another country or state?** *Chapter 12*

- My loved one died in one state but has a cemetery plot in another; how do I transfer the remains?
- Who do I notify if my loved one dies in another country?
- What is the best way to do this?
- What are airline rules?
- What are TSA's requirements for transporting cremains?
- Is it expensive?
- All of these questions and many more are answered in detail in *Chapter 12.*

Summary

No two funerals are the same. Each is complicated and filled with details. The hardest part is that it all can happen at lightning speed. This CHECKLIST aims to provide a valuable overview of different planning scenarios at the beginning of your journey so you can prioritize your tasks and choose the best people for each one. *The goal is to help you always keep the big picture in view.* This book has complete chapters on these bullet points to provide more in-depth information.

Hopefully, this CHECKLIST will save you valuable time and money and keep you focused and organized as you walk through funeral planning.

Notes

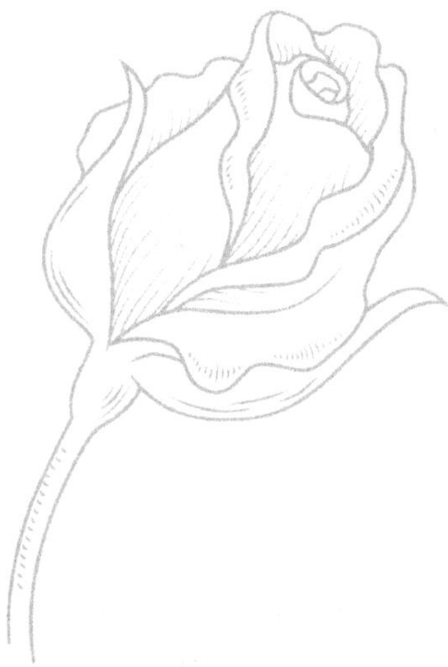

Chapter 6

Your Rights with Funeral Homes — *The Funeral Rule*

- *By refusing to think about death, we have been complicit in allowing the funeral industry to remain shrouded in mystery.*
- *The Federal Trade Commission's Funeral Rule has been written to regulate the industry and ensure consumer rights. However, you must know that this Rule exists to receive all the protections it affords.*
- *Informing funeral homes of your knowledge of the Funeral Rule lets the funeral director know you are an informed consumer. This may ensure more transparency in pricing or less pressure as you shop for goods and services.*

Think back to your hometown or neighborhood; you most likely can picture your local funeral home. They have always been bedrock members of every community. They were just there, usually large, well-kept pieces of real estate whose presence held a bit of mystique. The funeral director was just another member of your community, an important small family business. Everyone knew they would eventually need their services—but please—not today.

In many ways, it is our choice that the details of the funeral industry are shrouded in mystery. No one wants to think about their own death or the death of a loved one, so why would we research a topic we do not want to contemplate? Consequently, most of us have no idea what funeral directors do. When we need them, they quietly appear and perform several services we are unaware of in the midst of our heartache, and after a few days, they slip silently into the background, blocked from our conscious memory. Consequently, at the time of a death, we are often unaware of how much funerals cost, and given our emotional state, we don't have the capacity to analyze how this funeral will impact our finances going forward.

> ***Realistically, even if you could assess the cost of a funeral after a death, you can't decline their services or refuse to buy their products.***

So, how can you keep costs down in this time of unexpected loss as decisions confront you at lightning speed from every direction amidst the brain-numbing fog of grief? Once again, I recommend that you choose an *Advocate* to be your eyes, ears, co-decision maker, and business manager to help you navigate the process. Become informed by proxy through this person, who will look out for your interests at each decision point. However, for your *Advocate* to be effective, you must understand your rights by being aware of the Federal Trade Commission's *Funeral Rule*, as discussed in this chapter.

What is the *Funeral Rule*, and what are your rights?

The Federal Trade Commission (FTC), under the auspices of the federal government, has regulated the funeral industry via the *Funeral Rule* since it was enacted on April 30, 1984, and amended in 1994. The *Rule* has given you numerous protections when you plan a funeral. The FTC oversees strict guidelines by mandating a code of conduct for all funeral directors in the U.S. and providing explanations of consumer protections.

However, these rights are worthless if you do not know the Funeral Rule exists and do not obtain General Price Lists or take the time to study their contents.

It is important to know that you can refer to the *Funeral Rule* for information or file a dispute with a funeral home if you have a complaint. Likewise, knowing these rights and proactively approaching the funeral director as an informed consumer may prevent misunderstandings and ensure transparent pricing.

Purchasing a funeral is not like purchasing a home. Given your emotional state after a death, you likely don't know what you want or need or have any idea what these items cost, so it is possible you will accept whatever you are offered. After all, the funeral director is the expert on this matter, is he not?

The *Funeral Rule* and the *General Price List* (GPL)

There are three price lists for funeral pricing. Be sure to request all three when researching.

- ***The General Price List*** or (GPL) for funeral goods and services.
- ***The Casket Price List*** for caskets and urns.
- ***The Burial Container Price List*** for burial vaults and grave liners.

The FTC says: *Get a written, itemized price list when you visit a funeral home.* *The funeral home must give you a General Price List (GPL) that is yours to keep. It lists all the items and services the home offers and the cost of each one.*

When you visit a funeral home either at the time of need or as a shopper, the funeral director must present you with a *General Price List* on a printed sheet for you to keep. He cannot just show you a copy in a binder or on a tablet. This sounds like common sense. After all, if you go to a store to purchase a dishwasher, you see all of the merchandise displayed side by side with clearly marked prices listed on each one. This is the model we are accustomed to. Think of any category— food, clothing, tools, and even the car dealership. We know the cost of all of the items before we make our selection. However, if you walk into a funeral home, you will find that some businesses openly present their prices as they are required to by the *Funeral Rule*, and others try to conceal prices from you unless you specifically ask.

Likewise, if you request a pricelist via email, you may encounter roadblocks. Funeral homes can be evasive because the *Funeral Rule* does not mandate that they send out their GPL via email. However, if you walk through their door, they *must* comply. Know that it is your right to request a copy of the *Casket and Burial Container Price Lists*, but unlike a *General Price List*, a funeral director may withhold these until you are ready to purchase from his business.

Why are General Price Lists so important?

First, you are making a $8,000–$30,000 purchase. What other large purchase would you make without comparing prices from multiple vendors? However, if you walk into a funeral home without knowing your rights, the funeral director may show you his price list in a notebook or on a tablet or, more likely, will ask what services and products you are looking for and then present you with a sample invoice for what you discussed. By passively participating in this exchange, you have just forfeited your right to find lower-priced options, especially if you choose a package. At this point, if you do not possess a GPL, you will be unable to compare the package price to itemized prices, and you will never see all of the fine print, which includes their policies. Several people I know have experienced this, and so did Rosa when she began to pre-plan her own funeral.

My guess is that most people won't remember the figures shown on a tablet five minutes after seeing them, and it seems funeral directors count on that. You should know that you have the right to hold a paper *General Price List* in your hand and take it home with you. Be sure to insist on getting your copy. Remember, there is power in being an informed consumer, and it may change the playing field.

> ***You should also know that the funeral director is in violation of the Funeral Rule if he discusses prices or services with you and does not give you a copy of the GPL.***

The format of the *General Price List* (GPL)

The *Funeral Rule* sets rigid criteria for what must be included on all GPLs in the country. However, the funeral home is free to arrange the pricing however they see fit. I will be honest when I tell you that deciphering *some* price lists can be challenging, so I have developed the **Funeral Home Price Comparison Worksheet** in *Appendix B*, which gives you a guide on what to look for. *Think of it as a word search of funeral terms and then fill in the blanks with the prices from the GPL.*

What is in a *General Price List?*

Costs for the following:

- Transporting remains from the place of death.
- Embalming (must be listed separately).
- Other body preparation for a visitation or viewing.
- Transfer of remains to another funeral home.
- Direct Cremation
- Immediate Burial
- Use of facilities for viewing, visitation, or wake.
- Use of facilities for a funeral service (body is present).
- Use of facilities and staff for a memorial service (with no body present).
- Use of equipment and staff for a graveside service.
- Use of a hearse, limousine, or van.
- Pricing for a rental casket and liner.
- Purchase of an outer burial container or an alternative container for cremation.
- Costs associated with cremation—cremation with viewing, Direct Cremation, or package price(s) for cremation.
- Transportation to and from the crematorium.
- Cost of cremation and crematory fees.
- Costs associated with receiving or transferring a body to or from another funeral home. This is related to a death that occurs outside of the state or the country.
- Costs of interment if the funeral home owns a cemetery.

Why should I insist on getting a copy of a *General Price List*?

Truthfully, there are many benefits to obtaining a copy of this document. It can help you analyze and understand the prices of the goods and services you need to plan your cremation or burial. It also allows you to compare itemized prices to items within a "package" to see if you are truly saving money, and by requesting—or insisting on getting a copy— it notifies the funeral director that you are an informed consumer. *Most importantly, by obtaining* GPLs *from multiple funeral homes in your area, you have concrete numbers to compare prices and services from competitors.*

Here are ten benefits of possessing a *General Price List*:

1. It may reduce the chance of receiving "less-than-transparent" pricing.
2. It may reduce the upselling of goods and services.
3. You can compare itemized prices with package prices.
4. You can read all the fine print.
5. It means you can dispute your bill if you need to because you have both their pricing and policies in your hand and can prove "he said—she said" scenarios.
6. It allows you to compare price lists from competing funeral homes.
7. It allows you to fill in the **Funeral Home Price Comparison Worksheet** in *Appendix* B with actual prices of funeral homes in your area and compare "apples to apples" in your own home.
8. It alleviates some of the stress of making all decisions at the funeral director's desk and on his timeline.
9. It allows you to have a more detached co-decision maker be part of the process.
10. You can start planning a funeral before you meet with the funeral director.

The *Funeral Rule* ensures that you are informed of all fees, such as the *Basic Services Fee.*

The FTC says: "*The Funeral Rule allows funeral providers to charge a Basic Services Fee that customers have to pay. It includes services that are common to all funerals, regardless of the specific arrangement.*" https://consumer.ftc.gov/articles/ftc-funeral-rule

This fee includes overhead and the following duties of the funeral director including:

- Transporting your loved one from the place of death.
- Meeting with the family and planning the funeral.
- Securing necessary permits for burial or cremation.
- Gathering information, filing, and securing copies of death certificates.
- Preparing and submitting death notices or obituaries.
- Sheltering remains.
- Coordinating the arrangements with the cemetery, crematorium, or other third parties.

Transparent pricing

The FTC says: *Get price information on the telephone. "Funeral directors must give you price information on the telephone if you ask for it. You don't have to give them your name, address, or telephone number first. Although they are not required to do so, many funeral homes mail their price lists, and some post them online."*

As stated above, you may request funeral pricing over the phone. However, there is a risk that you may only get a snapshot price of whatever you ask for. For example, you might call and ask, "How much do you charge for a cremation?" There are numerous options for a cremation, and a funeral director would be on the phone for a long time explaining all choices and their variables, so they choose one—probably their least expensive option— and later, you may find that some items may be missing. If you think about it, a phone request cannot give you the full picture of all of the options in that category. It's like calling Amazon and asking for the price of "*a*" book. Also, note in the FTC report listed at the end of this chapter there is evidence that funeral homes do not always give complete or accurate pricing over the phone.

Some funeral homes may email you a price list, and some are starting to post prices online, but the FTC does not require them to do so. Note that transparency in pricing by a funeral home may indicate a quality, reputable business, but always be on the lookout for hidden costs.

Walking into a funeral home to secure a price list is your best option. Remember, you do not have to give your name or any personal information when you enter a funeral home and ask for their *General Price List*, and you absolutely do NOT have to sit for a conference. Simply being aware of this fact makes funeral price shopping significantly less intimidating. If refusing to give your name makes you uncomfortable, simply have a fictitious name available before you enter.

Purchase only the items you need and want

> **The FTC says: Buy only the funeral arrangements you want.** "*You have the right to buy separate goods (such as caskets) and services (such as embalming or a memorial service). You do not have to accept a package that may include items you do not want.*"
> https://consumer.ftc.gov/articles/ftc-funeral-rule

The *Funeral Rule* gives you the right to select only the goods and services you desire. This right is guaranteed whether you purchase at the time of death or are selecting pre-paid services. It is always your right to resist being sold products like embalming, high-priced caskets, or burial containers that you do not need or want, but you have to understand what is happening to resist. You also have the right to understand why you need each product and service that is listed in the GPL, what it includes, and how much it costs, informing you of the financial consequences of your choices.

Embalming

The FTC says: Make funeral arrangements without embalming.
"No state law requires routine embalming for every death."
https://consumer.ftc.gov/articles/ftc-funeral-rule

- The cost of embalming must be noted as a separate line item in the GPL.
- No state law requires embalming for every death; however, some states require embalming or refrigeration if the body is not buried or cremated within a specific time.
- Embalming may be required if a body crosses state lines or is shipped by air or rail.
- If some form of preservation is necessary, ask the funeral home if refrigeration is available.
- Refrigeration costs can also be substantial, sometimes as much as $500 per day.
- Funeral homes may have a policy requiring embalming if there is to be a public viewing.
- Ask for clarification regarding funeral home policy vs. state law regarding embalming.
- If there is no public visitation, you may ask for a private family viewing without embalming. This might be an option, especially if refrigeration is available.
- Not all funeral homes have access to refrigeration, but if they do, they are required to give you the option of refrigeration over embalming within specific time parameters.
- Refrigeration may be adequate if the funeral is local and the time from death to burial is relatively short.
- Embalming is not required for Direct Cremation or Immediate Burial.

Casket Price List

The FTC says: "See a written casket price list before you see the actual caskets. *Sometimes, detailed casket price information is included on the funeral home's GPL. More often, though, it's provided on a separate casket price list. Get the price information before you see the caskets so that you can ask about lower-priced products that may not be on display."*

- Caskets and urns are often not listed in the GPL but, more likely, are listed on a separate *Casket Price List.*
- Before showing you any caskets, the funeral director must give you a written *Casket Price List* of all the caskets they sell, including vendors and model numbers. This allows you to compare the same item with other funeral homes or online.
- Seeing this price list guarantees that you can see the less expensive caskets, even if they are stored in a back room or an outside warehouse and are not on display.
- Ask for this pricelist before seeing caskets if the funeral director does not offer it.
- Research shows that most people will select one of the first three caskets they are shown, but these will be among the highest-priced offered for sale.
- In a few instances, funeral directors refused to give me the casket price list when I requested the GPL, stating that it would be given to me at the time of need. They were within the parameters of the *Funeral Rule* because they are not required to produce that price list until they show you their inventory, and I clearly was shopping.

Burial Container Price List

The FTC says: "*See a written outer burial container price list. "Outer burial containers are not required by state law anywhere in the U.S., but many cemeteries require them to prevent the grave from caving in. If the funeral home sells containers but doesn't list their prices on the GPL, you have the right to look at a separate container price list before you see the containers. If you don't see the lower-priced containers listed, ask about them.*"
https://consumer.ftc.gov/articles/ftc-funeral-rule

If the funeral home sells grave liners, vaults, or other cemetery services, you must be informed at the time of purchase if the cemetery requires a grave liner.

- Outer burial containers are not required by state law anywhere in the U.S., but almost all cemeteries have a policy that requires them to prevent graves from caving in.
- You have the right to see the *Burial Container Price List* before viewing them so you know the range of prices for these items.
- If you do not see the lower-priced containers listed, it is your right to ask about them.
- Additionally, the cost of opening and closing the grave or for recurring groundskeeping fees at the cemetery may be handled by the funeral home or the cemetery directly. Be sure you understand the cost of each.

The FTC says: "*Some funeral providers present their outer burial container selections through a book containing photographs of the various containers offered for sale. If you choose this approach, you must incorporate all the information required for the OBC Price List into the book.*" https://www.ftc.gov/business-guidance/resources/complying-funeral-rule#required-itemized-prices-on-GPL

Cemetery or crematory fees

The FTC says: "*Get an explanation in the written statement from the funeral home that describes any legal cemetery or crematory requirement that requires you to buy any funeral goods or services*" https://consumer.ftc.gov/articles/ftc-funeral-rule

You must be informed in writing if policies require you to purchase additional goods or services, which increase your cost. These may include alternative cremation containers and burial containers.

Cremation and cremation containers

The FTC says: *Use an "alternative container" instead of a casket for cremation. "No state or local law requires the use of a casket for cremation. A funeral home that offers cremations must tell you that alternative containers are available and must make them available. They might be made of unfinished wood, pressed wood, fiberboard, or cardboard.*" https://consumer.ftc.gov/articles/ftc-funeral-rule

The funeral director may not require you to purchase a casket for cremation. This is a waste of money and may be harmful to the environment. A funeral home that offers cremations must tell you that alternative containers are required and must make them available.

- These containers may be made of unfinished wood, pressed wood, fiberboard, or heavy-duty cardboard.
- The container should not cost more than $300.
- Beware of funeral homes that encourage you to purchase expensive cremation containers. This may be a sign of other questionable practices. If the container costs as much as the cost of the cremation, take your business elsewhere, or at least challenge the funeral director for a less expensive option. *Chapter* 14

You do not have to purchase a casket or urn from the funeral home you are using.

> **The FTC says:** *Provide the funeral home with a casket or urn you buy elsewhere. "The funeral provider cannot refuse to handle a casket or urn you bought online, at a local casket store, or somewhere else—or charge you a fee to do it. The funeral home cannot require you to be there when the casket or urn is delivered to them."* https://consumer.ftc.gov/articles/ftc-funeral-rule

Knowledge is power. As indicated above:

- The funeral director cannot refuse to accept a casket or urn you bought online.
- They cannot charge you a fee for purchasing it from another vendor.
- They cannot require you to be there when the casket or urn is delivered to them.

I have heard of funeral directors increasing other costs if customers purchase a casket elsewhere. The *Funeral Rule* states they cannot do this, and if you possess a GPL, you can prove the stated cost of other items and search the *Funeral Rule* to prove to them that they are out of compliance.

Purchasing funeral or cremation packages from funeral homes.

The FTC says: "*Buy only the funeral arrangements you want. You do not have to accept a package that may include items you do not want.* " https://consumer.ftc.gov/articles/ftc-funeral-rule

---

You have the right to analyze the actual cost of "package" pricing

- Funeral homes may offer package pricing.
- If you choose a package price for a cremation or a funeral, be sure you get a GPL to compare the package price with the sum of the itemized prices of the items you choose.
- Be sure the package does not include things you do not want, like a reception, and includes all the items you need, such as a grave liner, crematory fee, or cremation container. *Chapter* 14

For instance, a funeral home can present a package price for funeral goods and services and say that it saves you $1,000, but how do you know that is true unless you have a *General Price List* to look up each item? I performed this exercise for you in *Chapter* 14. I discovered one package was missing, a burial container, which you would be forced to purchase in addition to the package amount. Another package was missing a cremation container, while another was missing the fee for the crematorium. In these cases, the package price actually costs more than buying the items individually. But you will never know this unless you obtain and analyze the prices listed on the GPL.

To assist you with this analysis, I constructed a **Funeral Price Comparison Worksheet** in *Appendix* B to simplify this process for you. This worksheet gives you a place to list the prices of the plan you choose and the ability to check off the items that are either included or omitted, as listed in the fine print. Conducting this exercise is the only way to ensure you have not been subjected to bait-and-switch tactics.

One more time: To secure accurate package pricing, you must visit the funeral home and walk out with a General Price List in your hand. This is the only way that you can confidently compare itemized prices with the items included in a package.

Beware: I found that it is common to see a post-funeral "reception" in the package prices of some funeral homes. However, if your church is providing you with a free reception, you might not want or use a reception provided by the funeral home that is priced between $1,000–$1,600. *However, if you plan to have a reception elsewhere, purchasing the package will be a waste of money*. The small print states:

No credit or refund will be issued if a consumer chooses not to use any good or service included in a package.

However, the statement of the funeral home's policy that appears on the GPL is not that legible. It is actually written in this very small 8-point font:

No credit or refund will be issued if a consumer chooses not to use any good or service included in a package.

However, you will never know any of this information if you:

- are overwhelmed with grief and let the funeral director determine what you need.
- never see or read a *General Price List*.
- purchase a package but never read the fine print to determine what is included or what is missing.
- are sure the funeral home would never take advantage of you at a time like this.

Optional goods and services

The FTC says: "*You may be charged for other services and merchandise, including costs for optional goods and services.*"
https://consumer.ftc.gov/articles/ftc-funeral-rule

The funeral director may charge you for third-party purchases that he makes on your behalf. These may include:

- Memorial cards
- Thank you cards
- Guestbook
- Flag and case
- Prayer cards
- Cremation jewelry
- Cross
- DVD of memories

Understand the costs associated with cash advances

> **The FTC says:** "*Cash advances are charged by the funeral home for goods and services it buys from outside vendors on your behalf.*"
> https://consumer.ftc.gov/articles/funeral-costs-pricing-checklist

Some funeral providers charge you their cost for items or services they purchase for you. Others add a service fee for their time securing these items.

- The *Funeral Rule* requires those who charge an extra fee to disclose that fact in writing but does not require them to specify the amount of their markup.
- The *Funeral Rule* also requires that funeral providers tell you if there are refunds, discounts, or rebates from the supplier on any cash advance item.
- If funeral providers do not know the exact cost of any cash advance item, they must give you a "good faith estimate" before purchasing on your behalf. These items can include:
    - flowers
    - obituary notices
    - pallbearers
    - officiating clergy
    - organist, soloist
    - military honors
    - police escorts

Before the final payment

> **The FTC says:** "*Receive a written statement after you decide what you want and before you pay. It should show exactly what you are buying and the cost of each item. The funeral home must give you a statement listing every good and service you have selected, the price of each, and the total cost immediately after you make the arrangements.*" https://consumer.ftc.gov/articles/ftc-funeral-rule

In other words, the funeral director cannot wait to give you the total price of an invoice at the time payment is required or until after services have been rendered. This policy allows you to reduce the goods or services you might choose before it's too late, especially if you are overwhelmed by the final cost.

> **The FTC says:** "*You must give each consumer a completed Statement at the end of the arrangements discussion. If arrangements are made in person, you should give the Statement at this time. Giving a consumer a copy of the Statement at the funeral or mailing it to the consumer at some later date does not meet the requirements of the Rule.* https://www.ftc.gov/business-guidance/resources/complying-funeral-rule#required-itemized-prices-on-GPL

This is a protection for you. Here, you might see unauthorized items on your invoice, so you can remove them before the item is used or the service is rendered. However, you may also see items listed on your invoice that might be missing from a package you have chosen. You will be shown their policies on the *General Price List* if you protest any of these fees. Unfortunately, this might be the first time you've ever seen it. If it's in the fine print and you've never read it—you lose!

> ***For your protection, consider having the funeral director sign the invoice stating that no additional items will be needed for your service once you have been given a final price.***

Here is a sample from the FTC of what you might see in the GPL regarding Direct Cremation or Immediate Burial:

Our charge for a direct cremation (without ceremony) includes basic services of a funeral director and staff, a proportionate share of overhead costs, removal of remains, transportation to the crematory, necessary authorizations, and cremation.

If you want to arrange a direct cremation, you can use an alternative container. Alternative containers encase the body and can be made of materials like fiberboard or composition material (with or without an outside covering). The containers we provide are fiberboard containers or an unfinished wooden box.

Direct Cremation

A. Direct cremation with container provided by the purchaser $ ____________

B. Direct cremation with a fiberboard container $ ____________

C. Direct cremation with an unfinished wood box $ ____________

Immediate Burial

Our charge for an immediate burial (without ceremony) includes basic services of a funeral director and staff, a proportionate share of overhead costs, removal of remains, and transportation to the cemetery.

A. Immediate burial with casket provided by the purchaser $ ____________

B. Immediate burial with an alternative container $ ____________

C. Immediate burial with a cloth-covered wood casket $ ____________

https://www.ftc.gov/system/files/ftc_gov/pdf/Sample1-general-price-list_1.pdf

Planning a funeral long-distance

If you are planning a funeral long-distance, you will find it difficult to get accurate pricing over the phone. Not having a mandatory policy that requires funeral homes to email price lists also imposes an unnecessary burden on families. It is common for family members residing elsewhere in the country to make calls from another state to determine which funeral home to use after a loved one has passed. The FTC found that the information given by funeral homes over the phone was often incomplete, occasionally deceptive, and sometimes in clear violation of federal law as imposed by the *Funeral Rule.*

> ***General Price Lists gathered in advance are the best tool for controlling the cost of a funeral. Use the Funeral Home Price Comparison Worksheet in Appendix B to compare and analyze pricing and protect your money!***

A solution to this problem

If the funeral home refuses to email their *General Price List*, ask relatives who live in that location to visit local facilities and gather them for you by walking into the ones you are considering before you arrive.

Funeral Home Compliance Quiz

Visit a funeral home and analyze how easy they make it for you to obtain a *General Price List.*

Use this point system when you visit funeral homes.

Assess 1 *point for each action*

- The receptionist:

  ________ Gives you the GPL, and you return to your car in less than five minutes.

  ________ Tells you she does not have any price lists at her desk.

  ________ Pressures you for your name and the reason for your visit.

  ________ Summons a salesperson from the back who comes forward and asks how they can help you even though you have already told the receptionist what you want.

- The salesperson: (1 *point for each action*)

  ________ Makes you wait for their arrival.

  ________ Moves you to a conference room or begins a sales pitch in the lobby.

__________ Arrives without a price list.

__________ Informs you that the price list is too complicated to understand.

__________ Begins to ask you what services you are looking for.

__________ Presses for your name, assuring you there will be no obligation on your part—just weeks of phone calls.

__________ Presents you with a sales brochure that does not have any prices but has a beautiful layout of the services they offer.

__________ Shows you prices on a tablet or in a binder that clearly belongs to them, but nothing for you to keep.

__________ Questions your choice for burial or cremation, but if you indicate any indecision between burial or cremation, the salesperson begins to steer you toward the more expensive choice—burial.

__________ Steers you toward a package or two while explaining the benefits of each, but never lets you see a print version with prices or the fine print or allowing you to compare the package price to the itemized prices—assess 10 points.

I have experienced each of these things at some funeral homes, and sometimes, almost everything on this list has happened at a single funeral home. Assess one point for each action and an additional 20 points if you leave their establishment with lots of paper, including beautifully crafted brochures including information regarding the *Funeral Rule*, but without their official *General Price List*. Assess an additional 50 points if they are rude at any point in your encounter.

List the total score of your experience ____________________

Can you figure out what a perfect score is? You guessed it— 1! Shop three funeral homes in your area. After visiting them and assigning a score for each, I am quite sure it will be easy to determine which funeral home you might like to use for your loved one or to make an appointment for a pre-need conference.

Funeral home accountability

Funeral homes cannot be held to account unless you possess a *General Price List*. They can easily give partial or misleading information over the phone and likely not get caught. A paper copy of a *General Price List* is the only way you can:

- know what they said.
- remember what they said.
- compare what they said.
- read between the lines of what they said.
- analyze what they said.
- prove what they said.

Speak out or speak up!

If you feel you have been overcharged or treated unfairly by a funeral home, resolve to break the code of silence! Tell everyone in your family, your friends, and your community what this funeral home did to you in your hour of grief! Consider posting your grievance on your social media! The FTC encourages you to file your complaint with the business itself, but if you feel their offense is egregious, you can file your complaint with the FTC. They will not address your case directly, but they will look for patterns among providers.

> ***However, if you feel you were treated compassionately and prices were fair and transparent, give feedback to that funeral home, tell your family and friends, and write them a positive review.***

In this industry, all funeral homes are grouped together. Those who run their businesses with integrity are harmed by those who do not. The only way to find the gems is to visit funeral homes before you need them. And the only way to shine a light on these compassionate businesses is to recommend them to your friends and give them positive reviews. May they prosper! We need them!

If you run a compassionate funeral home with transparent pricing, consider posting on your website that you will email your *General Price List* to all who request one, or go one step further and post all of your prices online. Encourage customers to visit your funeral home and speak with you so you can answer their questions and explain your services and philosophy without obligation.

If everyone who reads this book visits three funeral homes, then funeral directors across the country will sense a movement. Those who take advantage of consumers may become concerned that their practices will be revealed to the public they serve. However, those who run their businesses with integrity will celebrate these actions since it will illustrate their fair practices to the communities they serve, which may substantially increase their business. Fairness and transparency in funeral pricing should be universal. A grassroots effort to secure it will benefit both these upstanding businesses and our families.

I concede that no individual can single-handedly change this industry or lower the cost of funerals, but we can share our experiences, both good and bad, with those in our own family and our circle of friends. Let's approach this by assuming that all funeral homes are run with compassion unless they prove otherwise.

Summary

The FTC's *Funeral Rule* has given you the right to have transparency in the pricing of the goods and services you purchase for your loved one's funeral to ensure that there are no surprises on the final invoice. However, securing and verifying this information is something you likely cannot personally do shortly after learning of a death. You will need help navigating your rights during this time. Once again, this is the reason to enlist an *Advocate*.

Taking time to understand your rights can deter the funeral home from upselling you on items like caskets and limousines, smaller items like flowers and video presentations, and items you may not need, like a reception or an expensive casket for either burial or cremation. It can also inform you of the cumulative costs of extraneous small-ticket items.

If you are concerned about the cost of a funeral, address your concerns with the funeral director before you sign a contract. Being aware of the Funeral Rule and visiting two or three funeral homes at the time of death can result in finding a compassionate funeral director who will be sensitive to your needs *and* provide the most competitive pricing. Now imagine how much less stress you will experience if you have already visited funeral homes and made your selections prior to experiencing a death.

Imagine finding this funeral home. The message on the front of their brochure read, **"Pay Your Respects, Not Your Life Savings."** Wow! That was good enough for me to decide to use this funeral home.

It's time to get this done.

Addendum:

The FTC in action

On January 24, 2024, the FTC sent out a press release announcing that it had conducted an undercover phone sweep of funeral homes in 2023 encompassing all regions of the U.S. They indicated that they had surveyed 250 funeral homes and had subsequently sent out warning letters to thirty-nine funeral homes that were found to be in violation of the Funeral Rule. The headline read as follows:

Press Release: FTC Sends Warning Letters to Funeral Homes After First Undercover Phone Sweep. *Staff found that some funeral homes provided inconsistent pricing information while others failed to provide pricing entirely.*

However, these are only warning letters, and each states that no charges will be filed at this time for being out of compliance. So, even though a letter from the FTC to a funeral home should have the same impact on them as a letter from the IRS has on you, this problem that has an easy solution won't be solved.

> ***In this digital age, it would be simple for the FTC to require price lists to be emailed upon request, period. Until that happens, this slap on the wrist will likely lead to business as usual.***

Below is a summary I compiled from searching all thirty-nine warning letters on the FTC website. The violations include:

- "Failed to provide accurate information about prices or services by providing materially different prices on a telephone call than were stated on the *General Price List*." (NJ, MI)
- "Staff provided inaccurate information over the phone about its prices and offerings and misrepresented whether embalming is required by state law, code, or regulation."
- "Failed to provide accurate information about prices or services over the phone. The FTC contacted offices on two occasions and was provided materially different prices for the same goods and services on each call." (VA, TX, CT, CA, MA, PA, FL, OH, NC, GA, NY, FL, WA, ME, NV, AR)
- "Funeral home stated over the telephone that it would email a *General Price List*, but it emailed a list of package prices that did not meet the requirements for a *General Price List* under the *Funeral Rule*." (TX)
- "Failed to provide any information about prices or offerings over the telephone when asked." (D.C.)
- "Misrepresented that health codes require embalming before more than a limited number of individuals can view the remains, even if the remains are refrigerated." (AZ)

For the full article and the list of funeral homes found in violation, visit the website listed below.
https://www.ftc.gov/news-events/news/press-releases/2024/01/ftc-sends-warning-letters-funeral-homes-after-first-undercover-phone-sweep

Also, on the evening of January 25, 2024, CNN released an article on this subject entitled:

Government Warns Funeral Homes to Stop Misleading Bereaved Customers About Pricing by Ramishah Maruf, CNN (1/25/2024).

Here is the link to the CNN article: https://www.cnn.com/2024/01/25/business/government-warns-funeral-homes-on pricing/index.html

RESOLVING PROBLEMS

If you have a problem concerning funeral matters, it's best to try to resolve it first with the funeral director. If you are dissatisfied with the funeral services you receive, the Funeral Consumers Alliance offers advice on resolving a problem. In addition, the FEO, the NFDA Help Line, and the ICCFA Cemetery Consumer Service Council may be able to provide informal mediation of a complaint. You also can contact your state Attorney General's office or local consumer protection agencies.

In addition, you can file a complaint with the FTC online or call 1-877-FTC-HELP (382-4357) TDD: 1-866-653-4261. Although the Commission cannot resolve individual problems for consumers, it can act against a company if it sees a pattern of violations of the law.

Chapter 7

The Manner of Death Determines What Happens Next

- *Unexpected and tragic deaths contain unique and stressful challenges.*
- *This chapter discusses what you can expect if you are notified of such a death.*
- *Be sure to surround yourself with friends and family during this difficult and unsettling time.*

When a death occurs, a person must be officially *pronounced dead* by medical personnel, usually a doctor or a nurse. However, EMTs, police officers, and firefighters can also *declare a person dead*. Each state has statutes regarding who can determine if a person has passed. Once the pronouncement is made, your family will be contacted.

If the death is at home

You can call a funeral home directly, day or night, and a funeral director will pick up your loved one. However, your options will be limited if you have not gathered any pricing information before the death since you will need to have the body removed within a few hours. Once you call a funeral home, transportation fees and the *Basic Services Fee* will go into effect immediately, and your window for comparing prices is closed.

The situation is different in the case of illness or if a death is imminent. You still have the opportunity to gather pricing information from local funeral homes so that your decision will be made before your loved one passes. If you have decided to have your loved one cremated by a direct cremation facility, you will call the facility directly, rather than a funeral home, after your loved one passes.

If the death is in a hospital, nursing home, or hospice setting

Once you are informed of the death, you must first choose a funeral home or cremation facility, and your loved one will be picked up from that facility directly by your chosen funeral provider. You may only be given a few hours to vacate that facility.

If there has been an accident

Your loved one will remain at the scene until a medical examiner arrives to determine the cause of death. The police will investigate how the accident occurred. Was the death directly related to the accident, or was it due to a medical condition? This information is critical in the payment of insurance claims or in determining whether criminal charges will be filed.

Using a victim's ID and phone, the coroner or the police will attempt to identify your loved one and notify your family. When the coroner completes his initial investigation, the deceased will be transported to the morgue. Later, you may be asked to go there to personally identify them. If this is too traumatic for you, ask a relative or friend to accompany you. Once there, the coroner will definitively establish the cause of death and determine if further investigation is necessary. When all the facts have been gathered and all of the questions have been answered, your loved one will be released to your family. Once again, you will be asked which funeral home you would like to use.

If the death is a suicide

You should know that **suicide is not a crime**, but the police must be notified because it is considered an *unnatural death*. The police are required to treat the place of death as a crime scene. The authorities must be sure that someone did not stage the suicide to cover up a crime. Again, a medical examiner must be notified, and the procedures will mirror those listed above. In the first few hours, the police may limit your access to your loved one until they have completed their initial investigation. They may ask to take away some of your loved one's personal belongings, including notes, phone, or computer, for their analysis. Be sure to request an inventory for your protection so that all items are returned to you after the investigation is complete.

Again, someone will have to make a positive identification, and you will have to decide whether it will be you. The police may question you; try to be as helpful as possible, and feel free to ask for their discretion. On the other hand, it is your right to spend time saying goodbye to your loved one if you choose, and you may request that your loved one be covered to protect your last memory. All of this is difficult, but your wishes will be honored by the medical examiner. Note that the medical examiner may be required to perform an autopsy, and it is your right to obtain a copy of the report.

Here are some additional thoughts:

- **If the suicide is by gunshot**

  Call a professional cleaning company. The police will use chemicals and dust for fingerprints during their investigation, and they will not clean your home before they vacate it. They may either leave the body in place to be picked up by a funeral director or send it to the morgue for an autopsy. Your home now contains bloodborne pathogens and biohazards that carry harmful bacteria and diseases. Refrain from allowing friends or relatives to clean the space. They do not have the proper chemicals and may cross-contaminate your home.

- **Stay with relatives or friends during this time**

  A professional cleaning process may take a few days, so make other arrangements for your physical and psychological health.

- **Gather documents**

  Notify your homeowner's insurance company; they may cover some or all of the remediation of your home. Then, proceed to search for documents pertinent to death, especially those needed for the death certificate. This topic is covered in detail in *Chapter* 9.

- **Seek grief counseling**

  Suicide brings on complex emotions of confusion, guilt, and even betrayal. Don't try to navigate this by yourself. If you have children, everyone may need both individual and family counseling. Ask family and friends to help you find local or online counseling services. Your health insurance may cover this.

Be sure to visit the American Foundation for Suicide Prevention's website: https://afsp.org/ for helpful information during this tragic time. If you need help for yourself or someone you care about, **call 988**, the **National Suicide and Crisis Lifeline,** or text TALK to 741741. https://www.aftermath.com/content/suicide-crime-scene

If a person dies alone at home or foul play is suspected

Once again, an autopsy will have to be performed by a medical examiner to determine the cause of death before your loved one is released to a funeral home. The exception may be an elderly person who has been living alone. Important note: If the death is at home, no matter the circumstance, it is essential not to move the body until EMS, the police, or the funeral director arrives.

If the death happens away from home

If the death occurs out of state or even out of the country, the body must be flown back and then received by a funeral home. Another option is to cremate the body before transport and then move the cremains. This subject is covered in detail in *Chapter 12*. *(Note: Those who travel out of the country should consider purchasing insurance to return their remains to the U.S.—just in case).*

Summary

Death is cruel. No matter how we lose a loved one, we are never ready to let them go. It is as if a part of us has been carved away. No more hugs, no more intimate conversations, no more nuggets of wisdom, no more birthdays or holidays, or hearing their voice when the phone rings. And when we most need to be quiet, to process how our life will be different from this moment forward, the demands of the world go off like sirens, incessant and intrusive.

Do not walk this alone. Allow family and friends to help in the difficult times you will face in the weeks ahead.

Notes

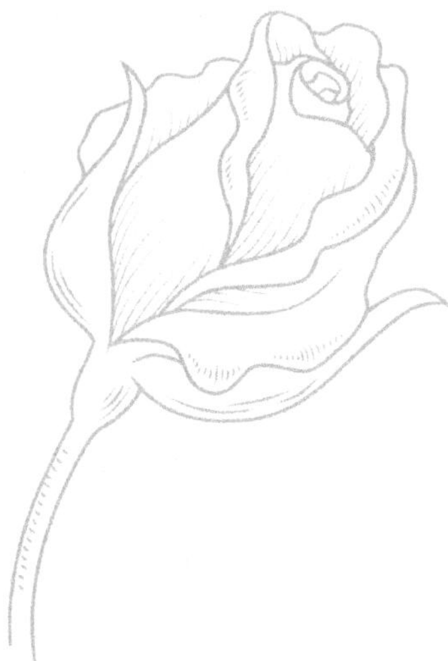

Chapter 8

Now it's Time to Plan: Will There Be a Visitation, Funeral, Memorial Service, or Celebration of Life?

- *Your decisions will be guided by your family's religious and ethnic traditions, as well as your personal financial situation.*
- *If cost is a concern, compare the information listed below to the pricing information in Chapter 14 or the timelier information your Advocate or family members have gathered from your local funeral homes.*
- *Many norms of past generations are fading, so feel free to customize your service.*

It is important to note that no two funerals are the same. Each is customized to reflect and celebrate a unique personality and a life well lived! Where will this service be? Discuss whether you will have a funeral or memorial service in a church or funeral home or a more secular service, often called a celebration of life at a funeral home or other venue. Contact your chosen location for a date and time. Be sure not to make formal announcements about your service until you receive confirmation of the facility's availability.

Should our service be in a church or funeral home?

Sometimes, family members charged with planning a funeral do not practice the faith traditions of their deceased loved one, and they may find it uncomfortable to plan a religious funeral. If you find yourself in this situation, here are some guidelines:

- Ask yourself who the funeral is for and what your loved one would want.
- I guarantee that the answer is that your loved one would want to be buried in the faith tradition they practiced.
- Be aware that all churches encounter this situation often.
- Understand that neither the pastor nor the staff will judge you or your choices. Their only focus is to lay your loved one to rest.
- Every church has a staff member or a team that handles funerals.
- You do not have to design the funeral. You simply have to make a phone call to the church office. They will meet with your family and lovingly guide you through the process.

Once, I encountered a family who had spent hours on the internet researching the format of how to plan a funeral in the faith tradition of their mother. They presented their plan to me, and I was able to accept some, but I could not integrate all of it. They could have saved themselves so much time and stress if they had just contacted the church at the time of death.

Funeral—memorial service—celebration of life

A **funeral** is a ceremony to honor your lost loved one with a body or cremated remains present with interment to follow.

A **memorial service** is a funeral ceremony without the body or cremains present. Sometimes, in the interest of time, this may occur while the body is awaiting cremation. Memorial services can occur within days of death or may be delayed for weeks or months.

A **celebration of life** is generally less formal and less solemn and often does not involve a religious service. It is typically held at a restaurant or venue with or without cremated remains, but it can also be held in a park, at the ocean, or on top of a mountain. However, you should note that some funerals and memorial services are sometimes also referred to as a celebration of life.

A **hybrid of these options.** Another possibility is a funeral celebrated with the body present in one location, and following the funeral, your loved one is taken for cremation. The interment or other ceremony with cremains may happen immediately after the funeral or weeks or months later, and sometimes in a different place. This may happen if an elderly parent has moved from their lifelong home to be near an adult child. The parent may have formed relationships in their new location, so they may choose to have a funeral or memorial service in their new home, but the children know that their mom or dad would prefer to be laid to rest back in their hometown in the family cemetery plot with their spouse. This may generate a need for a funeral in one location with a burial in a second.

Wake—viewing—visitation

These terms are used interchangeably; however, the term *wake* derives from 'watch' or 'vigil' and implies a more formal structure. It may be led by clergy and include prayers and Scripture. As late as the 1950s, wakes were sometimes held at the deceased's home. Family members remained awake and kept vigil with the deceased for two to three days until their loved one was taken to the church for the funeral and burial. By contrast, a *viewing* or *visitation* may be less structured, less formal, and likely not include a religious service. Regardless of what you call it, this is a time for family and friends to gather, pay their respects to the deceased, and offer condolences to the family. A casket is usually present if the person is to be buried.

In the present day, viewings and visitations are typically held at a funeral home or church. It is important to note that in some religious traditions, Buddhism—for example—the service may be held at the deceased's home.

The family decides if the casket is open or closed. An open casket makes the reality of the person's passing more concrete for family and friends and can be an important element of closure for the immediate family, especially if the death has been sudden. However, under certain circumstances, a closed casket is warranted.

The funeral director, family, or friends can lead the visitation or viewing service. Unfortunately, the additional cost of a viewing coupled with the rising cost of funerals and burials make this gathering expendable. Families often opt out of this extra expense and, in so doing, miss out on this valuable time to hear memorable stories of their loved one.

Having attended dozens of wakes/visitations over the years, I find that these gatherings are often more touching than funerals because of their informality. Gathering neighbors, friends, work colleagues, and extended family from far away gives the family the most consolation. They are often comforted by raucous laughter while listening to a humorous story that even the family has never heard. Husbands and wives have remarked that they learned something new about their spouse of thirty years at the wake. This gathering is a chance for everyone to say a final goodbye and demonstrate to children or spouses the far-reaching impact their loved one has had upon the world. If you are celebrating the funeral in a house of worship, it may offer its facilities to you for this purpose without cost. Other places of long-time affiliation may do the same. Try to make this happen; it is a precious step in the grieving process.

Evening calling hours allow work colleagues and persons with time constraints, such as young mothers, to attend and offer condolences and support to their friends, even if they cannot attend the funeral. It allows guests to introduce themselves to all family members and share how they are connected to the deceased. If you are expecting a large number of people to attend the viewing, a receiving line may be in order. Funeral homes can accommodate these gatherings, but churches have recently assumed this role to help families cut costs.

Friends can find the date, time, and location of the visitation and the funeral from a death notice or obituary in a newspaper, the funeral home's website, or by calling the funeral home or church. Try to gather this information online or from friends, the church, or the funeral home rather than calling the family.

A sample format for a wake or viewing:

Note: A memorial video slideshow may run continuously during the service.

6:30	Private visitation for the family (*sometimes, this is the only time the casket is open*).
7:00	Visitation is open to the public.
7:15	A short prayer service if you are following a religious tradition. (*Optional*)
7:30	Memories and stories shared by guests where everyone is invited to speak.

Wake, viewing, and visitation etiquette

- These services may last for hours, and attendance for the duration is neither expected nor required.
- If the body is present, the casket is open, and you are uncomfortable, you are not required to look at it or approach the casket.
- If you wish to view the body and pay your respects, choose a time when no one else is doing so.
- Once your private moment is complete, do not linger or engage in conversation near the deceased since others may be waiting to pay their respects.
- Before you leave, find a few moments to offer your condolences to the family. If you have not met previously, take a moment to introduce yourself and explain your relationship to the deceased. Keep this exchange brief, as others may be waiting to do the same.

Funeral in a church setting

The role of the clergy is to offer comfort, prayer, and counsel during this difficult time. If your loved one follows a religious tradition, embrace the reassurance and structure that its rituals can provide. In the case of illness, contacting the pastor, priest, or rabbi before or immediately after death is appropriate.

Most religious traditions have a general outline for their funeral service that includes a time and a place for a eulogy. When you contact the church, you can discuss the format used in their faith. It is customary to offer an honorarium to the clergy after the service from $150–$300 for the funeral, plus additional stipends for a wake or service at the cemetery. Note that the music is often live, and musicians also have fees; sometimes, they are included on your funeral invoice, but in other instances, they are paid directly by the family. Be sure to ask your funeral director for clarification.

Once your family has decided to hold the funeral in a church, contact the church office. You may meet with the pastor or designated staff member(s) responsible for funerals. They will discuss what you need regarding dates and facilities. You may receive materials that will help you choose music and Scripture. *(If you are planning your own service, there is a list of common Scripture citations in* Appendix E *that apply to any Christian setting.)*

You will also receive assistance in choosing music and securing musicians. Ask if the church or funeral home will provide a program for the service or if you should prepare your own. There is a template for this in *Appendix D*. It might include a picture of your loved one, an obituary or tribute, a scriptural text or poem, and an outline of the service, including the page numbers of songs or hymns. If family members participate in the service, their names should also be included.

Ask about the church's guidelines for a eulogy, its placement in the service, and the rules for placing flowers in the church. Understanding the church's policies is essential so that you do not order expensive arrangements that may not be used. If cremated remains are present, there will be a table to display a framed photo of your loved one and your loved one's cremains at the front of the church and another table for a photo and guest book in the gathering space, so you may need two photos.

Funeral at a funeral home

This service can have a casket, cremated remains, or no body at all. The service can be religious, with invited clergy officiating, or completely secular, led by a friend, family member, or the funeral director. Music may be recorded or live. Readings may be Scriptural or inspirational. Guests may be invited to speak about your loved one, and a eulogy may be delivered. The time frame should be about sixty to eighty minutes. Guests have given you part of their day to honor your loved one, so be sure to respect their time.

A celebration of life at a venue

This will be a party. Choose a restaurant, reserve a hall, call a caterer, or make it a potluck. Place a framed photo, guestbook, and flowers at the entrance. Prepare a table at the front of the hall, including a framed photo with flowers and, if you like, the urn. Cremains may or may not be present at this celebration.

Plan to have family members speak on behalf of your loved one. Consult the chapter on eulogies to set up guidelines for speaking. You may also invite friends to speak extemporaneously, but this should be preplanned with time limits and controlled by a master of ceremonies. A memorial slideshow may run in a loop on a projection screen. Be sure to introduce all family members that participate. Keep it joyful but respectful.

A graveside service that replaces a funeral

A graveside service may serve as a final farewell for the family and close friends if there is no formal funeral. This service can be for the burial of a body—Immediate Burial—or the burial of cremated remains—Direct Cremation. The funeral director, a member of the clergy, a family member, or a friend can lead this service. There may be recorded songs and an inspirational message or Scripture reading. A family member may read the obituary or give a eulogy. You may invite friends to speak to offer tributes or tell stories. Remember, weather can be a factor in graveside services. Some cemeteries will provide a tent, but generally, it is just large enough for your family. Brevity may be the order of the day.

Reception

Many funerals are held in the late morning, and some churches provide a meal prepared by volunteers for family and guests after the funeral or memorial service if you or your loved one is a member of their community. Churches may or may not charge for this, but donations are appropriate for table settings, drinks, plates, etc. Most churches do not charge for the facility if you are a registered member of their community; however, a donation to the church will be graciously accepted.

Other options include a meal at a restaurant or someone's home, often for immediate and extended family. This allows the family to remain together longer in an informal setting. It also may include family members who have traveled just for the funeral, sometimes from significant distances, and may not have seen each other for a long time. This can be a heartwarming gathering and should be planned if possible. You may have heard family say they only see each other at weddings and funerals. Unfortunately, in our complicated world, this may be even more true today than in the past, but these events provide the ties that bind families together.

Summary

The circumstances in the days following a death will vary widely depending on two factors— whether or not the death was expected and whether or not you have made a plan. If you have never thought about death, you will be forced to make almost one hundred decisions in the thirty-six hours after hearing the news while trying to cope with your loss.

> ***If you have made a plan, you or your family can comfort each other while you walk through your grief, and the decisions regarding the logistics of the funeral will almost execute themselves. I'm sure you'll agree that executing a plan is much easier than making and executing a plan.***

If you have suffered a tragic death, you most likely will scarcely remember anything from the moment you received the news of the death through the funeral. Let yourself be taken care of by friends and family during this time. Enlist your *Advocate* and your family to handle the funeral and burial logistics and only bother you with crucial planning and financial decisions.

> ***You can choose to do this either proactively or reactively. The decisions are the same, but but the burden on your family is vastly different.***

By now, you can see that there are unlimited possibilities for your loved one's send-off, and there are various ways to personalize a final farewell. It can be elaborate or simple, religious or secular. The only requirement is that it reflect the uniqueness of the deceased, your family, and your traditions. Customize it for your family, make it memorable, and include everyone. Fill all ceremonies with your family stories, traditions, food, and lots of love. Let this time be a warm embrace for your family amid these difficult circumstances.

Remember, only a few people in the world know you—each other—and share the same stories. They are your family!

Notes

Chapter 9

The Death Certificate

- *A death certificate is an official legal document issued by your state that verifies the deceased's identity and confirms the death.*
- *Death certificates are required to handle personal, financial, and legal matters of a person's estate.*
- *This process also notifies the Social Security Administration of the death.*

A *birth certificate* confirms your birth and identity while you are alive. It allows you to generate a Social Security Number or replace a Social Security card. You need it to register for school, obtain a driver's license, a passport, and apply for a marriage license. In the same way, a *death certificate* is vital for closing out your life. It confirms that you have lived and allows others to conclude your unfinished worldly business.

What is a death certificate?

A death certificate is a government-issued legal document that confirms a person's death, verifies their identity, and permits a family or other legal entity to close out the deceased's affairs. Most states use The Centers for Disease Control and Prevention's U.S. *Standard Certificate of Death.*

Who must sign the *Standard Certificate of Death*?

- The medical examiner, coroner, or licensed physician who pronounced the person dead signs the document—*to attest to the death.*
- The medical person who examines the body and describes the date, time, location, and cause of death signs—*to certify the death.*
- The funeral director who verifies the deceased's identity, gathers personal information from family members, including the deceased's Social Security Number, describes the disposition of the remains via burial or cremation, and files the certificate with your state—*registers the death.*

Finally, medical and statistical information regarding the death is sent to The National Center for Health Statistics (NCHS) in the offices of the CDC.

Why do I need a death certificate?

When most people die, they leave a lot of unfinished business behind. The death certificate proves that you have lived and are now deceased. It acknowledges that you probably had family, money, real estate, and financial obligations. All of these things have to be closed out. Possession of the death certificate gives your family members or an executor of a will the authority to conclude your worldly business.

From the moment of your death, the state takes great care to verify who you were, how you died, the disposition of your remains, and who is entitled to your money and your property. Like your driver's license, Social Security Number, passport, signature, fingerprints, and now your facial recognition verified your identity when you were alive, the care taken from the moment of your death not to lose track of you is manifested by the death certificate. It becomes your proof of death for all of your unfinished business, financial and legal affairs.

Information needed for the death certificate may vary from state to state. The minimum information required is:

- Name of the deceased
- Date and place of birth
- Date and place of death
- Most recent address
- Father's name
- Mother's maiden name
- Social Security Number
- Cause of death

Many states also require the following:

- Marital status
- If male and married, the surviving spouse's maiden name
- Ethnicity
- Age
- Gender
- Location of death—home, hospital, nursing home, etc.
- Name and address of the funeral home and funeral director recording the information
- Method of disposition of the body—burial or cremation
- Whether the deceased served in the U.S. Armed Forces
- Highest level of education
- Occupation and type of business/industry in which the deceased worked

What is the funeral director's role in creating the death certificate?

The funeral director:

- Obtains the signature of the physician or medical examiner who has examined the body and determined the time and cause of death.
- Obtains the personal information listed above from the family.
- Reviews the certificate for completeness and accuracy.
- Delivers the completed form to the local city or county reporting authority.
- Notifies the medical examiner or coroner of any death he believes was due to accident, suicide, or homicide if he moves a body from a non-medical facility such as a home or other private facility.
- Cooperates with state or local registrars concerning queries on certificate entries.
- Cooperates with pathologists in cases involving postmortem autopsies.
- is thoroughly familiar with all laws, rules, and regulations governing the federal vital statistics system.
- Calls on local officials or the state office of vital statistics for advice and assistance when necessary.

If the death is not local or is a homicide, the funeral director completes and files the certificate of death according to the state's laws in which the body was found.

> ***The Social Security Administration is automatically notified of the death when the death certificate is filed with the state. You may need to visit them if, after the death, you become eligible for benefits or your benefits change.***

What is your state's role in issuing a death certificate?

- All of the information on the *Standard Certificate of Death* is sent to your state's vital records office for review.
- Once documented and input into their system, officials issue the original death certificate.
- This original document is kept on file in your state's vital records office.
- *A death certificate is always issued in the state where the death occurred.*

What is a *certified copy* of a death certificate?

- A state official in the vital records office with access to the original death certificate must verify its authenticity before creating certified copies with an official embossed state seal.
- The embossed seal makes the death certificate difficult to reproduce.
- These certified copies can only come from the state.

How do I get copies of the death certificate?

- The state will send a single death certificate or the number you ordered directly to the funeral home, and the funeral director will notify you to pick them up.
- This is the only time the funeral director will order copies for you.

> ***The funeral director does not keep a copy of death certificates on file. After the funeral, it is your responsibility to order all future copies from the state.***

What is the difference between a *certified copy* of a death certificate and a *copy* of a death certificate?

- A copy is just that, a photocopy of a certified copy that is used for informational purposes.
- These copies do not include an *original government seal* and are considered informational rather than legal documents.

Should I make a digital copy of a death certificate?

- You can so that you will always have one available, but it will be a copy of your certified copy and will not be accepted as a substitute for financial, real estate, or government transactions requiring a certified copy.

The following entities require certified copies of a death certificate:

- Social Security Administration—to claim survivor benefits.
- Veterans Administration—to notify and claim benefits, including burial in a Veteran cemetery.

- Local probate court—to appoint an executor or administrator of a will and initiate the probate process.
- Insurance companies—to notify and secure benefits *(one copy will be needed for each company)*
- 401Ks and retirement plans—to access funds.
- Military benefits—to claim benefits for surviving family members.
- Banks—to access accounts, to redeem treasury bills and IRAs, and to access a safe deposit box.
- Credit card companies—to cancel credit cards.
- IRS—to file the final federal tax return.
- State tax office—to file the final state tax return.
- Courts—to transfer deeds and titles, to sell real estate or vehicles, or to transfer a business.
- TSA—to transfer human remains if traveling by plane.
- Brokerage accounts—to transfer, redeem, or liquidate securities or investment accounts.
- Unions—to secure benefits.
- Pension providers—to suspend payments and claim final benefits, including insurance.

How many copies of the death certificate do I need?

- Order one copy for every account you find: banks, mortgage companies, Social Security, insurance policies, pension plans, investment accounts, deeds, titles, and credit cards, to name a few.
- If you need to change it or close it, you will need a copy of the death certificate. Think 15–20 copies.

The following entities *may* accept a photocopy, scan, or fax of a death certificate. *Be sure to call before you go.*

- Credit bureaus—to file a notice of death.
- Deceased's employer—to notify, claim benefits, and final entitlements.
- Membership, subscriptions, or service providers to cancel services.
- Homeowners and car insurance companies to process insurance claims, change payee, or terminate the policy.
- Professional offices—to close files and cancel future appointments.
- Passport office—to cancel a passport number; however, the family may keep a passport as a memento.

- Health care providers—to cancel coverage.
- U.S. Post Office—to transfer, forward, or cancel mail service.
- Local court—to certify that a spouse has passed so the surviving spouse may remarry.
- Cell phone provider—to cancel service.
- DMV—to cancel a driver's license, which may prevent identity theft.
- Employers of family members to file for bereavement time. https://www.joincake.com/blog/who-needs-original-death-certificates/ Sam Tetrault B.A. English 12/15/22

Who can request death certificates? *(This may vary from state to state)*

- Parents
- Legal guardians
- Spouses
- Children
- Grandchildren
- Siblings
- Executor of the estate
- State and federal agencies for official purposes

In some states, death certificates are considered public domain documents and can be obtained by any entity or individual requesting them.

How long does it take to get death certificates?

The funeral home must file the death certificate with the county health department within three to ten days of death. The state vital statistics office will handle the death certificate processing, which usually takes ten to twelve days, and they will send the certified copies you ordered back to the funeral director. The state then forwards the information to the National Center for Health Statistics (NCHS). This agency records the information in a national database.

How do I get a death certificate if my loved one dies out of the country?

- When a U.S. citizen dies in another country, the U.S. embassy or consulate should get a death certificate of notification from the foreign government where the death occurs.
- The U.S. Department of State will then issue a *Consular Report of Death Abroad* (CRDA).

- This CRDA will be the proof of death in the U.S. and will serve as your death certificate for closing accounts and handling legal tasks.
- You can get up to twenty free certified copies at the time of death from the State Department. Be sure to request all twenty.
- A person who is considered the closest next of kin can request CRDAs.

How important is accuracy in gathering information for a death certificate?

Statistical data derived from death certificates can only be as accurate as the information provided on the certificate. All persons involved with the registration of deaths must strive for accuracy, promptness in reporting, and completeness.

Since death certificates may take several days or weeks to be returned from the state, local authorities use the above information to issue a *certificate of disposition of remains*, also known as a burial or cremation permit. The cemetery or crematorium requires these certificates as another link in the chain of custody of the body. Providing an accurate death record is the funeral director's responsibility as a service to the decedent's family and as the cornerstone of the nation's death registration and statistical data. https://www.cdc.gov/nchs/data/nvss/handbook/2019-Funeral-Directors-Handbook-508.pdf.

How is statistical data from death certificates used?

- Government officials review causes of death to determine if foul play was involved.
- Statistics from death certificates are also used to compile data on crime, car accidents, and gun-related deaths, to name a few.
- Public health officials use death certificates to identify public health problems and to compile data identifying disease trends, including leading causes of death. Public health policies depend on mortality data from death certificates to design effective public health programs. They are the primary source of information about the cause of death or the illness that preceded it. Public health departments could not perform their duties without this data.
- Mortality statistics are of considerable value to physicians and medical science because they can identify disease trends, evaluate diagnostic techniques, and determine areas of concern and funding for medical research.

- Demographers use mortality and birth and death statistics to estimate and project population sizes, which is essential in forecasting trends, planning programs, and budgeting.
  https://www.sciencecare.com/blog/death-certificate-need-one

Although the death certificates differ somewhat from state to state, they all contain:

- Information about the deceased and their family ancestry.
- Information about the disposition of the body.
- Certification by the physician, medical examiner, coroner, or another person legally authorized to certify the death.
- Information about the cause of death.

Summary

A death certificate is an official legal government document that declares the cause of death, the location and time of death, and other vital personal information about the deceased. Death certificates are filed locally with the county, registered by the state, and finally sent to the National Center for Health Statistics (NCHS). They are required for personal, financial, and legal matters in settling an estate. This includes accessing money, closing accounts, claiming benefits, filing tax returns, and transferring property, to name a few.

Some businesses may ask you to bring a certified copy of the death certificate to their location, and after seeing it, they will make a copy for their files and return the certified copy to you. Having an employee see the original or a certified copy verifies the death, and making their own copy is adequate for them. They also know that certified copies of death certificates cost money, and this verification method shows consideration for you. Carrying both certified copies and photocopies to appointments may be prudent, saving you time and frustration.

Producing a death certificate verifies the death and gives you the authority to inquire about and close the affairs of the deceased.

Notes

Chapter 10

Obituaries and Eulogies

The Obituary: A Written Searchable Legacy

- *The information in your obituary will be posted and retained by websites and newspapers for decades.*
- *Your loved one's obituary will be the legacy future generations seek as they attempt to piece together their heritage.*
- *A eulogy is the last living testament uniting the present with the past.*

Taking the time to craft a thoughtful, comprehensive, and accurate obituary is a demonstration of respect for your loved one. It may be the most lingering, searchable legacy of their life and your family for generations to come.

Although writing an obituary seems like another impossible task in your already challenging week, according to www.legacy.com, "an obituary acknowledges your loss, informs your community of the death, and invites those who knew your loved one and those who care about you to attend the visitation and funeral to offer sympathy and support." It tells the story of the deceased and lists a lifetime of accomplishments, including personal, professional, and community achievements. It also chronicles your family tree, both living and deceased.

Funeral homes, churches, obituary websites, and social media platforms enable you to publish an obituary online for free. Still, people will have to know where to look, so activate your social media network or email contacts to get the word out. Since the obituary will contain visitation, funeral, and cemetery information, including dates, times, and addresses of these places, it must be written in the first twenty-four to thirty-six hours after death.

Obituary websites are popular platforms for posting obituaries as our digital world expands. They are becoming more comprehensive as time passes, including guestbooks and video tributes. Some even allow you to create a memorial in addition to an obituary. They also may have a section to gather tributes from family, friends, and co-workers from around the country or around the world. These sites may even have a fundraising section for family or close friends. www.joincake.com

It can feel daunting to write an obituary, so please don't feel you must do it alone. Many families begin to write obituaries before they are needed, and some seniors write their own. Check with older family members if you need help recreating the family tree of those who came before you. If you still have time, ask your loved one what they would like included in their obituary before they pass.

The essential elements of an obituary include the following:

- **Death announcement**
    - First, middle, and last name, including maiden name, nickname, and suffixes like Jr. or Sr.
    - Age (optional)
    - Date and place of birth, marriage, and death
    - Cause of death (optional) may be listed to indicate a battle with a long illness, to raise awareness of a disease, and sometimes to reduce the number of times you have to answer the question, "How did your loved one die?"
- **Photo**
    - A recent photo or a photo from their youth
    - Find a clear, flattering headshot
- **Life story**
    - Places they have lived
    - Schools attended and degrees earned
    - Places of employment and positions held
    - Military service and rank
    - Community contributions
    - Awards and memberships
    - Place of worship
    - Hobbies or special interests
- **Family members and significant others**
    - Related family members, including a spouse, parents, children, siblings, grandparents, grandchildren, great-grandchildren, and those who died previously.
    - Extended family like nieces, nephews, aunts, uncles, cousins.
    - Those who are important but may or may not be related, including a fiancé, significant other, close friends, a devoted caregiver, and even pets.

- **Service information**
    - Important service information, including date, time, and location of the visitation, funeral, memorial service, and cemetery information for the community.
    - Indicate if the services are private.
- **Donations**
    - Flowers—assume family and friends will send flowers unless directed to do otherwise.
    - Scholarship fund.
    - Charity—your family may choose charities for friends to make donations rather than sending flowers. Be sure to include envelopes or website information to make this option convenient for donors. Include the name of the charity, its address, or a website where donations may be sent. Consider a QR code at the visitation for donation convenience.
- **Crowdfunding solicitation**
    - Funding to cover the cost of funeral expenses—this is the best time to do this. *Chapter 15*
    - Determine your crowdfunding source. Fill out a profile telling your story and post the amount of money you are trying to raise; include the information in your obituary and hope for the best.

The obituary can be posted online, in a newspaper, on a funeral home website, on Facebook, or on other platforms of your choice. Ideally, it should be posted at least two days before the funeral service. Once this information is released, people will begin to send flowers or make donations in honor of your loved one to the crowdfunding entity or charity of your choice, so these decisions need to be made early in your funeral planning process.

Understanding the cost of a newspaper obituary

Be sure you understand the cost of an obituary before you write. Your funeral director will inform you of newspaper deadlines and contact the newspaper directly but understand there will be a fee for this service. It is important to know that newspapers charge per column inch, line, or total word count, and city newspapers are more expensive than community newspapers. Since obituaries can get expensive quickly, it is important to understand the pricing rules of the paper you are writing for. A better approach may be to determine how much you want to spend and then limit the length of your tribute.

Other cost variables include the number of days the obituary will run or the days of the week you want it printed. An average obituary in a large city can cost between $200–$500. Originally, obituaries were always published in newspapers, and *geneologybank.com* is the most comprehensive newspaper obituary website in the U.S., with obituaries dating back to 1690. If the deceased was a long-time member of another community, possibly in another state, you might also consider sending the notice to that community newspaper.

A death notice is a less expensive option; it is short and to the point. It includes the full name of the deceased, including a maiden name, date, location of death, names of surviving family members, and details of the funeral and burial, including date, time, and place. If someone you know has recently passed away, you can search www.everloved.com by city to find obituary information, leave condolences, or even add a loved one's obituary.

Summary

As you can see, gathering details for an effective obituary is complicated, and it may be best to include many family members in assimilating educational, employment, community involvement, and the correct spelling of your lineage information. Assign an elder in your family to list names and dates, especially those in previous generations and the deceased's contemporaries. Starting this process before death is beneficial if the death is somewhat anticipated by age or illness.

Taking time to craft a thoughtful, comprehensive, and accurate obituary is a demonstration of respect for your loved one. It may be the most lingering, searchable legacy of their life and your family for generations to come.

The Eulogy – A Living Testament to Your Loved One

- *A eulogy is a last living testament uniting the present with the past.*
- *A eulogy is an oral testimony of remembrance. Its purpose is to pay tribute to your loved one.*
- *It is a seven to ten-minute summary of your loved one's footprint in the world.*
- *It can be delivered at a visitation, funeral, memorial service, celebration of life, or graveside service.*

Take time to tell the stories

The eulogy is a living biographical legacy of your loved one's life, family, contributions, and accomplishments. It is how we share this everyday person's untold stories. It can be formal or informal, serious or humorous. Take time to reflect on their personality. Choose one or two family members to write it. Tell your listeners how important this person was to you, your family, and their community, and how they will be missed now that they are gone. Incorporate lessons learned or favorite quotes that reflect the personality and character of your beloved. The writer should take notes as family members gather, share stories, and recall memories as well as personal and professional accomplishments.

There are good and bad eulogies. I have listened to hundreds of eulogies, and some of the best ones I've heard were so well organized and well delivered that I genuinely wished I had known the person in life! Even as a detached bystander, I have asked for a copy. You definitely want to take the time to write one of these.

Here is a formula for success:

- Opening: Introduce yourself and your relationship to the deceased at the beginning of your remarks. Remember, work colleagues and caretakers may never have met you. Old family friends or neighbors may not have seen you since you were ten, and they want to know who is speaking.

- Thank all who brought you to this point: guests for coming to the funeral, caretakers, hospice workers, neighbors, relatives, or anyone who has helped your family through the past few days, weeks, or months.
- Share the accomplishments of your loved one and any qualities or traits that made them unique and exceptional human beings. Share memorable family stories. Share personal quirks or the catchphrases that you heard over and over. Share stories of how they impacted your life, the person you have become, or their community. Don't be afraid to be funny—humor is endearing.

Here are the most important things in delivering a eulogy:

- Type it out and number the pages. Give a second copy to another person—just in case.
- Multiple family members can speak, but the eulogy needs to be structured and typed out in advance, regardless of how it is delivered.
- Keep it to five to seven typed pages, double-spaced, and no longer than five to eight minutes.
- Don't repeat things.
- Family members who are most comfortable speaking in front of a group should make the presentation. Being a little nervous is to be expected.
- Don't worry about being somewhat emotional; almost all eulogies are delivered by real people who choked up at some point in the delivery. However, getting choked up once or twice differs from falling apart. If you think this may be possible, excuse yourself from this task.
- The person who writes the eulogy does not have to be the one who delivers it, but the reader needs to practice and speak the words as if they are their own.
- Find a secluded place to practice saying the words out loud at least five to ten times. Use a large font, double-space your document for ease of reading, and put significant words in bold print.
- Try to make eye contact with your audience.
- Don't be afraid to use your finger to keep your place on your sheet. It gives you more confidence when looking up from the page.
- Connect with your listeners.

- Speak the words from your heart; don't just read them. Pause for emphasis or to let people laugh after a humorous thought.

A friend shared his eulogy for his father with me. Near the conclusion of his tribute, he moved toward his father's casket. As he placed his hand on it, his phone rang. He took the phone out of his pocket, looked at it, and excused himself, saying, "I have to take this." He listened for a moment, spoke softly to the caller, and after concluding the call, he related to the guests that it had been his father who called and had told him to "wrap things up." He reported that everyone had a good laugh as he brought his thoughts to a close.

Here are some of negative characteristics of eulogies you may choose to avoid:

- Not being prepared is disrespectful to both your loved one and your audience.
- Speaking spontaneously without a script or rambling demonstrates a lack of planning.
- Several people speaking and all saying the same thing shows you did not take the time to organize or coordinate your remarks.
- Speaking too long dilutes the message and may make your guests uncomfortable.

> ***It is a great honor to be asked to write or deliver a eulogy. After all, it may be the last public testament to your loved one's life and legacy. Plan it with care and deliver it with love.***

Summary

Eulogies and obituaries are important documentation of the life of your loved one. They are current events for your family now but will be a valuable part of your family story, history, and legacy in the future. So, take time to gather correct information about family names and relationships, both past and present. Listen to family stories and be sure to be accurate about dates of birth and death. Use this opportunity to record and share your family legacy. After the eulogy is delivered, share a written copy with your close family members so it can be passed to children, grandchildren, and cousins from the rest of the family tree.

At this moment in all of time, you are connected to your family to remember and honor this one significant person in everyone's life for the last time. Life will be different for each of you from this moment forward!

Notes

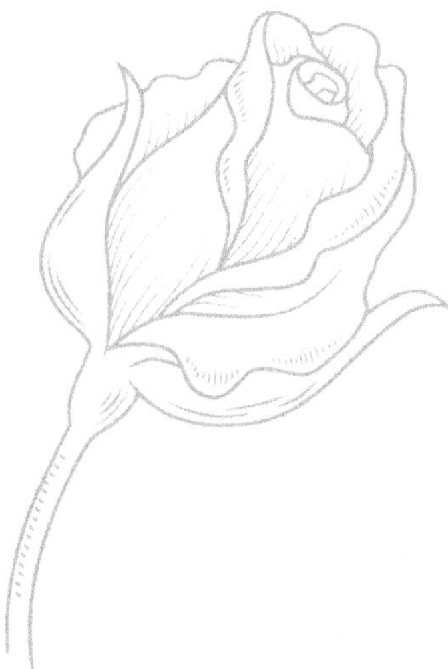

Chapter 11

Planning the Little Things

- *Once you decide how your loved one will be laid to rest, where the funeral will be held, and the kind of service you want, dozens of other decisions must be made.*
- *You can incorporate all or some of the items and ideas mentioned in this chapter to personalize your funeral.*
- *If cost is a factor, take time to determine what is important to you and dismiss the rest.*

Flowers vs. donations to a charity

Discuss with your family whether you want to receive flowers or have donations made to a charity like the American Heart Association, American Cancer Society, American Lung Association, or other research entity, or even the SPCA if your loved one was an animal lover. You can also consider setting up a scholarship at an educational institution to honor your loved one.

If you choose donations to a cause, it is generally up to the family to provide flowers for the service while offering friends the opportunity to donate to the cause. State your preferences in the obituary or online. Be sure to provide a URL for direct connection to the charity's website or include envelopes at the visitation or funeral to accommodate these gifts. You may also choose to solicit donations to pay for funeral expenses. Remember, people from out of town who cannot attend the funeral may still choose to donate; be sure to keep them informed.

Types of arrangements *(For your reference, these are 2024 prices)*

Half casket spray **$250–$350**

A half-casket spray is an arrangement that covers the lower part of the casket. This arrangement is best for a viewing when the casket is open. The spray will be delivered directly to the funeral home. Note: I cannot resist commenting on this expense. If you are having a large evening visitation, a service at a funeral home, or a service in a Protestant church with a closed casket, this arrangement may be worth the cost. However, if the visitation is short or occurs immediately preceding the funeral, these flowers may be on display for less than one hour. They may be removed at the church, left at the cemetery, or thrown away. It seems that purchasing a free-standing basket for your church to use during the funeral and for weekend services may be a better use of your money. I think this is a purchase that is always recommended because "that's what has always been done." So, consider if the cost is worth it for your family when making your decision.

Free-standing funeral sprays **$130–$300**

An arrangement is placed on a free-standing wire rack. Family, close friends, or a group of co-workers often purchase them. If there is to be a visitation, these arrangements will always be sent to the funeral home or, if not, directly to the church.

Floor basket arrangement **$ 80–$150**

A large triangular or round floor arrangement that is often placed in the sanctuary of a church.

Funeral standing basket **$100–$200**

Close family or very close friends, a group of acquaintances, or co-workers usually send these baskets. Local florists create these arrangements with seasonal flowers, and they are sent to the funeral home if there is to be a viewing or directly to the church if there is no viewing.

Funeral flower bouquet **Various prices**

These arrangements are perfect for sending to the family's home to let them know you are thinking about them during this difficult time. Friends and co-workers often send funeral bouquets to support family members they know personally.

Funeral plants **Various prices**

Family, friends, or co-workers may choose to send plants instead of a bouquet. Plants serve as an ongoing reminder of both their loved one and the kindness of the giver. Often, these plants are sent to the funeral home, but they might be best sent to the recipient's home to prevent loss or damage as they are moved from the funeral home to the service and then to the cemetery, where they may be left behind.

Things to consider

Arrangements for the service are usually purchased by the family. They may be included in your funeral package price or purchased from an online florist like 1-800 *Flowers* or a local florist.

Before ordering flowers, consider the space in which they will be used. Consult with the funeral home or the church where you will hold your service to determine the best arrangements for their space. I have often seen expensive arrangements left unused in the back of the church because they did not fit in the space or interfered with the religious tradition.

How do you order flowers for a funeral?

- Ordering flowers for a funeral may differ from a typical floral delivery order since it is very time-sensitive. You will need the name of the deceased and the address of the funeral home or church, as well as the date, time, and location of the visitation or funeral.
- Decide on the arrangement you would like to have delivered. A variety of funeral arrangements and flower bouquets can be created. Use the selections listed above or browse floral websites.
- Craft a message for the card. Take a moment to write a personal, heartfelt message to your relative, friend, or co-worker. Be sure to give your name or the name of the individual or group sending the arrangement.
- A local florist will deliver the order directly to the funeral home or church.
- To save money, you can research a local florist in the city of the funeral and call them directly to eliminate an online service fee. Sometimes, you will even get free delivery if the funeral home or church is in their delivery area.
- In large urban areas, multiple funerals can be at the funeral home at the same time, so providing accurate and complete information ensures that your arrangement will arrive to the correct recipient on time.
- Plan to have someone retrieve smaller arrangements after the funeral to give to family or friends. Otherwise, they will be left at the church, funeral home, or cemetery and thrown out.

Choose burial garments

If your loved one is to be buried, you must decide what clothing you want them to wear for burial. It may be a military uniform, or a dress worn at a significant event. You may also include jewelry, a special memento, or a book. In the case of a child, you may want to place a toy or a blanket in the casket, but you need to consider this carefully before you permanently part with the item. Keeping the memento at home may give you more consolation during this sorrowful time and for years to come.

What about cremations?

Some cremations have both a viewing and a funeral service before the cremation, and funeral flowers are considered an appropriate gesture at either event. If you are unsure what you should send, check with either the funeral home or a member of the immediate family for guidance, or consider sending an arrangement or a plant to their home.

How to handle condolence calls

There will be many calls to your family when friends, neighbors, or co-workers learn of your loved one's passing. It is appropriate to have a relative or close friend screen these calls by documenting the person's name and phone number so that you can return or acknowledge the calls at a future time. Some callers may call for information; others may offer help or food. It is appropriate for these volunteers to assist you by returning calls, answering questions, accepting food, or assigning tasks such as soliciting a car to drive your out-of-town guests to the funeral, cemetery, or reception.

Memorial card

This card will have a picture of your loved one on the front, the date of birth and death, and a poem, prayer, or Scripture quote on the back. These are important family keepsakes; they are small and can be kept in a drawer, so family members are likely to keep them. You can purchase them through the funeral home or make your own and have them printed on card stock and laminated at a local office supply store, or you can purchase them online. These cards are often one of the few mementos that may be passed down through generations, so keep the leftovers. They may be found after your passing and will provide important generational information for your children and grandchildren. I suggest you don't skip this step.

Guest book

A guest book will be included if you use a full-service funeral home; otherwise, be sure to purchase one. Be sure to ask before you make this purchase. It is a log of the people who have honored your family by attending the viewing or funeral service. Commonly, one or more immediate family members will miss seeing or speaking to an attendee. This book will provide valuable memories for years to come and be helpful as you consider writing thank-you notes in the coming days.

Pallbearers *(only needed if there is a casket)*

Pallbearers are generally men, but women can also be named. These individuals accompany the casket from the hearse onto a rolling dolly. Their function is to escort the casket down the aisle of a church as the funeral begins and reverse the movement at the end of the service.

Pallbearers should not be directly connected to those most impacted by the death. For instance, a son-in-law may need to support his wife if the deceased is her parent or sibling. The people you choose for this role can be family members, such as nephews, grandchildren, friends, or even business colleagues.

Customarily, six pallbearers are needed to carry the weight of the casket. Honorary pallbearers can also be chosen. Generally, these may be older persons who are not required to carry any weight. In certain circumstances, there may be a need to hire pallbearers. The funeral director can usually do this for you.

In some cases, pallbearers may be required to carry the casket physically. Caskets can weigh 250-350 pounds or more. Before you accept this honor, be sure you understand what the funeral home and the cemetery will expect of you. We had a situation in my family where only four strong young men were available. They needed to carry the casket a distance of ten yards from the hearse to the gravesite and then lift and place it onto a strapping cradle above the grave. The combination of weight, distance, and movement over uneven ground at the cemetery almost led to a disaster.

A note to pallbearers

As a pallbearer, you should wear a jacket and tie, dress pants, and comfortable dress shoes that are not slippery (*no athletic shoes*). You should turn off your cell phone from the moment you begin your service. This will ensure that you are not tempted to look at incoming messages. The role you have been given is one of honor, and it is important that you give your deceased loved one your full attention and respect for a couple of hours. The funeral director will provide complete instructions on how to carry out your function.

Reception

After the funeral, it is common to have a reception. It may be provided by your church, family members, or friends. Sometimes, all guests who attend the funeral are invited, and at other times, this reception is only for family. It may be at a restaurant or someone's home. There is no right or wrong way to do this. Do whatever is comfortable for the principal mourners.

House sitter during the visitation or funeral

For home security, you may decide to designate someone to remain at the deceased's home during a wake or funeral service. This task might be appropriate for a neighbor or co-worker who is connected to you rather than to the deceased and wants to help. It is common for criminals to search obituaries to learn when a home will be vacant. Consider if this is needed in your area.

Memorial video presentation

The funeral home has traditionally provided this service, but in recent years, as technology has advanced, many families now create their own. Gather memorable family photos of your loved one through the years and create a slide or video presentation. This presentation can be shown at the wake/visitation, the funeral, or even the reception. Remember to share copies of this with other family members as a perpetual family memorial.

Transportation

Another way to save money is to reduce the use of funeral home transport vehicles. For instance, you may choose to decline the limousine and only use the funeral home hearse to transport the casket. Transportation for family members to and from the church or to the gravesite may be by friends or, in most cases, other family members who drive their cars. You may also need a vehicle to transport flowers. Funeral homes charge a fee for all vehicles used. Be considerate of those from outside the area, and ensure they have the correct addresses for the church, cemetery, or reception so they do not miss any events. Consider asking friends to transport guests from out of town to the church or cemetery.

Funeral service program

If you expect several guests to attend the funeral, you might want to consider a program for the ceremony. It should list the order of service, including Scripture citations, hymn numbers, music unique to the faith tradition, and any family or friends who may be serving. A program is an inclusive gesture that allows universal participation. This is a nice touch for guests who may not know the family members or may not practice your faith. A program is also appropriate for a more secular celebration by listing the order of the events and the names of the participants.

You can use plain copy paper or purchase specially printed covers for funerals. The size could be an 8½ by 11 sheet of paper folded, or a better choice might be an 8 ½ x 14 sheet folded. The cover could have a picture of your loved one, their name, date of birth and death, the name of the church or funeral home, and the funeral date. The inside could have the order of the service with all participants listed. It could include the cemetery location and information about the reception if guests are to be invited. *I have enclosed a template of a funeral program in* Appendix D.

Thank you notes

Thank you notes are important. Friends, neighbors, and co-workers may have made financial donations, sent flowers or food, or traveled a great distance to show how important you and your family are to them. Using your guestbook, make a list of attendees and assign someone to find addresses. Delegate one or more people to write these notes. If it was a large funeral, you can come up with the sentiments and have friends or family members help write and send them. For instance, the same sentiment can be sent to all co-workers who made donations or sent flowers and another to neighbors who brought food. Even if you purchase customized notes, each should include a short two to three-sentence personal message. Do not forget clergy who may have assisted you.

Most of these items are available through your funeral director. You can also visit the website www.funeralprints.com for a wide variety of printed keepsakes, including custom-designed prayer/memorial cards, obituary bookmarks, funeral programs, thank you cards, guest books, and commemorative posters. The site also includes helpful ideas for designing your items.

Summary

I've included this chapter to give you an overview of the typical elements of a funeral, which will hopefully help you organize and prioritize your tasks and find the right person for each one. If the death has been unexpected, you may need more help navigating the process. If you are a family member, your skills can be utilized in several ways to ensure all goes well. If you are a close friend, you may have a clearer head to assist with planning. Don't hesitate to volunteer your services and your time.

Funerals are complicated and filled with hundreds of details. Make your celebration unique in a way that honors both your loved one and your family.

Notes

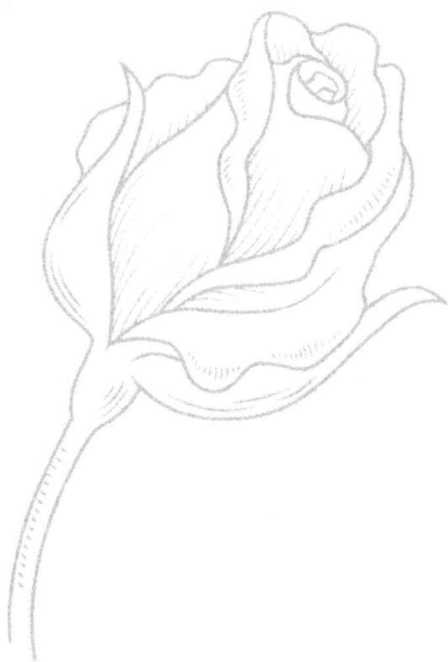

Chapter 12

Transporting Remains

- *If a death occurs in another location, returning your loved one home can be complicated and costly.*
- *This chapter will suggest strategies for what must be done if the death is in the next town, another state, or a foreign country.*
- *This topic has numerous variables, so I have provided basic information and listed my sources so you can explore the areas pertinent to your situation in-depth.*

The era of living in the city or town where you were born for your whole life and dying there seems to be disappearing with the World War II generation. People relocate for work, children relocate after college, and seniors leave their generational homes later in life to be closer to adult children and their grandchildren. This migration has created another anomaly. It is no longer uncommon for people to die in one location and be buried in another. In addition, Americans are more mobile than ever. They travel domestically and internationally for work and pleasure, while many may live abroad for years for work or during retirement. This chapter addresses the challenges of this mobility, including moving remains or cremated remains from one location to another.

Transporting a body within the U.S. either by vehicle or by air

- This scenario is common enough that the FTC has required it to be listed on the *General Price List* of every funeral home in the country. The categories are *Forwarding Remains to a Funeral Home*, and *Receiving Remains from a Funeral Home.*
- The funeral director will obtain a burial transit permit. This records the deceased's cause of death, their personal information, your contact information, and the release documentation needed to transport remains. The laws of each state may vary. Visit the following website to check the funeral laws of any state https://www.nolo.com/legal-encyclopedia/home-funeral-laws
- Transporting remains is a costly service. For example, prices on GPLs were $4,000–$5,800 to forward remains and $2,900–$3,700 to receive them. The forwarding fees are higher because the body needs to be prepared and may have to be embalmed.
- The cost for ground transport of a body to and from an airport could be $300–$500 each way if the death is near a large airport. The cost could be higher if smaller local carriers are necessary, and the distance to the airport is significant.
- Funeral homes and transport services may charge $3.00–$5.00 per mile.
- In rural areas where a major airport may be hundreds of miles from the place of death, and sometimes even in another state, I saw one airport transit fee of $1,200. Transportation of remains is often higher in a rural area. If you encounter this situation, you will have to pay both forwarding and receiving fees to each of the two funeral homes,

plus the cost of transportation, which could rise to almost $10,000 or more, before you begin planning the funeral.

Where do I begin?

- Contact a funeral home in your location to receive the body. They will contact a funeral home where the death occurred to arrange for release.
- In some cases, the body may have to be embalmed within forty-eight hours before a transfer. Be sure to check the regulations for your situation.
- Since the death certificate is not yet available, the funeral director must secure a *burial transit permit*. This records the deceased's cause of death, their personal information, your contact information, and the release documentation needed to transport remains. Laws from each state may vary. Visit the following website to check the funeral laws of any state. https://www.nolo.com/legal-encyclopedia/home-funeral-laws
- During this time, you should contact the airline that you wish to use.

Can I use my vehicle to transport a body?

There are several considerations for this type of transfer.

- You will need a vehicle that can safely transport a casket.
- Check state regulations regarding transporting the deceased both within your state or across state lines.
- The body may have to be embalmed and placed in a casket or valid transport container.
- The driver must be legally allowed to transport remains in every state you drive through.
- A burial transit permit may be required.
- Be sure to carry the death certificate and death registration documents with you.

Professional ground transit:

Depending on the distance, a professional ground transit service or a funeral home may arrange transportation. They will likely charge you $3.00–$5.00 per mile.

The shipment of cremated remains

With cremations on the rise, it is possible to relocate your loved one after death by carrying cremains on an airplane or by mailing them through the *U.S. Postal Service*. These options are not common dinner conversations, but it is important to be aware of them either at the time of death or as you make your final plans.

Can I transport cremated remains on an airplane?

Yes, you can transport cremains on a plane, but here are some guidelines to make this transfer uneventful.

- The TSA recommends choosing a transport urn made of biodegradable materials like wood or plastic. The remains must pass through a TSA scanner. If your urn is made of a dense material like metal or stone, the agent may not be able to see into the container, and you may not be allowed to proceed. Note: *The final decision rests with the TSA officer on whether an item is allowed through the checkpoint. It will do no good to demand to see a supervisor if your container is refused.*
- Consider purchasing a low-cost travel urn to keep the remains secure and allow TSA agents to determine what is in the container to clear it for travel. It is illegal for TSA agents or any airport personnel to ask you to open the sealed container containing cremains, and they will refuse to do so even if you ask them to do it. But TSA agents must be able to see into your container with their scanners to ensure the security of all items brought onboard an airplane.

> ***Unfortunately, misrepresenting contraband as cremated remains is one of the many tactics used by persons wanting to conceal a dangerous or illegal item during a flight.***

- If the TSA agent cannot verify the content, they can refuse to clear you for travel. https://www.memorials.com/tsa-approved-urns.php.
- Be sure to order your TSA-approved urn early enough so a delay in its arrival will not interrupt your travel plans.
- Another way to avoid delays is to choose a temporary urn with a "flight ready" label. This urn is guaranteed to pass through security and has the proper labeling for flight. These containers are available on Amazon or Etsy.

- Each airline has its own policy. Some allow urns to be transported in carry-on baggage, and some do not allow urns in checked baggage. If permitted, consider using a carry-on so your loved one will remain with you even if your luggage is lost. It is best to contact your airline to determine their policy and criteria before you get to the airport.
- Give yourself plenty of time to pass security. If you are stopped, you may have to ship the remains, which may result in missing your flight.
- Be sure to bring the *death certificate* and *certificate of cremation* plus proof of your relationship to the deceased, possibly a copy of the obituary, in your carry-on luggage. While this will not guarantee passage of your urn, it may assist you if there are questions from TSA agents or airline employees.

Can cremains be shipped within the U.S.?

- Yes, the **U.S. Postal Service is the only legal way to ship cremated remains**, and this may be a more stress-free solution than flying with cremains.
- The USPS now has two *Cremated Remains Kits* available free of charge from the *Postal Store on* USPS.com.
- These kits are not available at local post offices. Please read USPS Publication 139 from the USPS for all packing and shipping requirements. www.about.usps.com/publications/pub139.pdf
- These packages must be shipped via Priority Mail Express, costing $25–$30. This method includes tracking to prevent loss. Your loved one's cremains will usually arrive at the destination within two days. Also, note that funeral directors may charge $100–$200 to provide this service for you. Some funeral homes may require you to purchase a mailing container from them; however, the container is free from the USPS. If cost is a concern, save yourself $150. The USPS has made this easy for you to do yourself.

> ***To be clear and save you time—UPS, FedEx, and other carriers DO NOT ship cremated remains.***

Something to consider

Since transporting cremains can be relatively easy within the U.S., and you know how expensive burial plots can be in urban areas, it might be reassuring to know that a plot your parents or grandparents purchased fifty or seventy-five years ago is available to you and your family in their hometown. If the plot has already been purchased, transporting cremains might be an option worth considering; the cemetery staff will help direct you. In a more rural area, you can be buried for the cost of digging the grave, which could be $100–$200, rather than the cost of $3,500 for a plot plus $2,700 in opening and closing fees in your current city of residence.

Can cremains be shipped internationally?

- Yes, they can, also by the U.S. Postal Service. The rules depend on the country of death or the country of entry.
- If remains are shipped to a foreign country, check with the destination country's consulate or embassy to ensure you comply with all of the regulations of that country.
- The shipping cost can range from $50–$300, but it might be cheaper than buying a last-minute plane ticket because TSA or your airline has held you up for non-compliance with their regulations.
- Also, note that some airlines may not allow cremated remains either onboard or in checked luggage.
- How often have you changed carriers or had a luggage delay in an emergency or weather situation? Shipping may be your most stress-free option.
- For additional information, see *Transportation and Safety Administration (TSA) Ways to Travel with Cremated Remains* or call TSA at 1-866-286-9673. https://www.tsa.gov/blog/2018/07/10/ways-travel-cremated-remains#

What is the first call I should make if my loved one dies overseas?

If you have an emergency overseas, your first call should be to the **U.S. Department of State's Overseas Citizen Services.** Call: 1 (888) 407-4747 if you are in the U.S. or Canada, or 1 (202) 501-4444 from outside of the U.S. to contact the nearest U.S. embassy or consulate. You can call 24 hours a day. travel.state.gov

Note that the U.S. government does not pay for the repatriation of a deceased U.S. citizen. All costs are the responsibility of the family.

- Hospitals and local police will notify a U.S. embassy or consulate of the death of a U.S. citizen.

- The rules regarding death are different for each country, but the U.S. embassy or consulate in the country of death can assist you in sending instructions to the correct offices in a foreign country.
- The embassy or consulate will assist you with exchanging U.S. dollars into local currency, and the consulate in the country of death will help you disburse the funds to pay for the repatriation.
- If there is no family in the country of death, the consular officer, following local law, may take possession of jewelry, documents, papers, and clothing of the deceased for safekeeping. They will create an inventory of the items and then carry out the instructions of the next of kin or legal representative of the deceased.
- The U.S. consulate in the country where the death occurred will assist you in making arrangements with local authorities and finding an experienced local funeral provider for cremation or repatriation of a body to the U.S.
- It is important to use the services of a professional funeral company in the country where the death occurred that specializes in international preparation and shipping of remains.
- The consulate will prepare a mortuary certificate in English called the *Consular Report of Death Abroad* (CRDA) which includes the cause of death and other related information, to ensure compliance for shipment and clearance of U.S. Customs.
- You should understand that there are fees for the consulate to process paperwork and documents that facilitate the repatriation.
- If the death has occurred in a remote area, you may need to use an international assistance company, such as International SOS or First Assistance, to act as an intermediary with an international funeral director.

What is a *Consular Report of Death Abroad* (CRDA) and why is it important?

When a U.S. citizen dies abroad, the death is reported to the U.S. embassy or consulate in the country where the death occurred. In their official capacity the embassy or consulate:

- Confirms the death, identity, and U.S. citizenship of the deceased.
- Attempts to notify the next of kin.
- Obtains a copy of the local foreign death certificate from the country where the death occurred.

- Coordinates with the family regarding the deceased's remains and personal effects.
- Provides guidance on how to forward funds to cover costs.
- Serves as a provisional conservator of the estate until the legal representative or family member arrives.
- Prepares documents for the disposition of remains according to the will of the deceased or the family.
- Assists in finding a foreign funeral home confirmed as one that complies with the regulations of the country where the death occurred and coordinates with U.S. Customs, airlines, and a U.S. funeral home for the transfer of human remains.
- Sends electronic or paper copies of the *Consular Report of Death Abroad* **(CRDA) which will serve as the death certificate** for the next of kin or legal representative to use in settling the estate in the U.S.
- Will issue you an electronic PDF of the CRDA upon receipt of the foreign death certificate. The document contains the digital signature of the consular officer and the digital seal of the U.S. embassy or consulate. You are permitted to make as many copies as you need at the time of receipt or at any time in the future.
- Will issue up to twenty paper copies of the CRDA at the time of death at no charge.

It is important to note that the U.S. embassy cannot finalize a CRDA until the foreign death certificate is issued, which may take from four weeks to six months, depending on the country where the death occurred. https://travel.state.gov/content/travel/en/international-travel/while-abroad/death-abroad1/consular-report-of-death-of-a-u-s--citizen-abroad.html#

> ***The CRDA is used as proof of death in legal proceedings in the U.S. and functions the same as a death certificate in settling estate matters since there is no U.S. death certificate***

My loved one died overseas, and I want their body returned to the U.S. What can I expect?

> **The chain of custody of a body must always be between two government-authorized legal funeral representatives, both nationally and internationally.**

- Contact the **Department of State's Overseas Services at 1 888-407-4747.**
- Contact a funeral home in the U.S. that is certified as a "known shipper" to receive the remains. This funeral home must register with each airline it uses and is certified to comply with TSA's guidelines for shipping and receiving human remains.
- The U.S. funeral home must contact the consulate in the country of death to determine local procedures and find a local authorized provider to ship remains in the country where the death occurred.
- Air transport of remains happens daily, but it must be done through authorized funeral homes at both the point of origin and arrival.
- The airline's mortuary cargo fee is calculated according to the weight and the distance between the point of origin and the destination. Expect to pay between $2,000 and $6,000 for transport. Most airline carriers have a limit of 500 pounds, that is, the combined weight of the remains and the casket. If the combined weight exceeds this limit, there will be an additional cost. www.US-Funerals.com
- There can also be an international ship-out fee, starting at $3,000–$4,000, in addition to the airline fee.
- Embalming may or may not be required, depending on the country you are shipping from.
- The shipping cost of cremated remains internationally will be approximately $300, while shipping a person's body can cost $10,000–$20,000, according to International Insurance. https://www.insuranceiig.com/

What if my loved one is a citizen of a foreign country and dies in the U.S., and I want to transport their body back to their home?

- Contact a local funeral home in your region that is a "known shipper." They follow all procedures to prepare a body for shipment as required by U.S. Customs, TSA, and your chosen airline.

- Before the transfer, you must obtain a U.S. death certificate from your state.
- The U.S. consulate in the receiving country may be able to assist you in finding funeral homes authorized to receive the remains.
- You may have to contact the consulate or embassy in the destination country to learn about that country's specific legal requirements. There may be forms that require authorization or translation.
- Call airlines that travel to that region to discuss their rules regarding such a transfer.

What if my loved one died overseas, and I want to have them cremated before bringing them back to the U.S.?

- Having your loved one cremated in the country where the death occurred is much simpler and more affordable than transporting a body internationally.
- Direct cremation may cost $500–$1,500, depending on the country.
- Then contact the airline you intend to use to discuss their policy for traveling with cremated remains.

What documents must accompany the deceased during transport?

The laws of each country will determine the documents that are required. Regardless of the country of death, all documents must be translated into English.

- You will need a foreign death certificate which becomes the *Consular Report of Death Abroad* (CRDA). This is the legal document that serves as a U.S. death certificate and is used to settle all estate matters in the U.S.
- From the U.S., you will need a U.S. death certificate issued by the state where the death occurred.
- Embalming certificate or cremation certificate.
- Consulate documentation.
- U.S. Customs import/export documentation.

If you have chosen to transport the body of the deceased, and the remains are not embalmed, the consulate will alert U.S. Customs and provide the following:

- A consular mortuary certificate.
- An affidavit of a foreign funeral director.
- A statement from foreign authorities on the cause of death.
- Transit permits if ground transportation has been required.

Summary

If you or your family members travel regularly, have relocated for work, or have moved from your city or town of birth, leaving parents behind, or if your children do not live where you do, you may have to confront relocating remains at some point in your life.

Each year, over 6,000 U.S. citizens die abroad. Most of them are Americans who live overseas, but a percentage are Americans who are on vacation. It is reassuring to know that U.S. embassies and consulates have the personnel to assist you through the process if death abroad happens to you or your family.

The ease of transporting or shipping cremains gives you the option to reduce the cost of relocating your loved one's remains after death.

Notes

Chapter 13

Navigating Funeral Traditions of Religions and Cultures

- *We encounter diversity in our lives every day, and when our friends and co-workers experience a death, we want to support them, but we may be unsure of what to do.*
- *Each religion and culture has meaningful traditions and rituals surrounding death.*
- *This chapter gives you an idea of what to expect at a funeral for someone of a different culture or religion and guides you in funeral etiquette and attire.*

Understanding religious and ethnic cultures can help us offer our condolences while not violating protocols. Most Christian religions have funerals within a week, but Jewish and Muslim funerals are held as soon as possible after death. Buddhist and Hindu cultures have a structured and much more extended mourning period. Here are some guidelines to help you navigate this time of mourning for your friend or colleague. Be sure to check out the websites listed for much more detail regarding funeral rites, traditions, and etiquette.

Protestant funerals—General

- Christian funeral services with burial commonly occur at a church or funeral home within seven to ten days of death.
- There may or may not be a viewing before the funeral.
- A minister will conduct the service with participation from family members.
- *What to do for all denominations:* Visit the funeral home during scheduled visiting hours and/or attend the funeral.
- *What should you send:* Flowers, cards, food, and charitable donations in the deceased's name are appropriate expressions of your sympathy.

Methodist funeral

- It is preferred, but not required, that the body be present at the funeral.
- If the family chooses cremation, it should occur after the funeral.
- *The Service of Death and Resurrection* is a prescribed outline for a funeral service found in the United Methodist Hymnal. It includes prayers, Scripture, and hymns. https://www.umcdiscipleship.org/book-of-worship/a-service-of-death-and-resurrection

Lutheran funeral

- It is preferred, but not required, that the body be present at the funeral.
- The casket is covered with a white cloth called a pall.
- The church follows a formal liturgy service, including a gathering rite, prayers, Scriptural readings from the Old and New Testaments, the Apostle's Creed, the Lord's Prayer, and hymns interspersed throughout.
- The funeral itself focuses on the faith life of the deceased.

- It is preferred that a eulogy or other non-religious tribute occur at the visitation or the reception following the funeral.
- There may be a Communion rite offered during the service, and all attendees of any faith are invited to participate. https://irp.cdn-website.com

Presbyterian funeral

- The funeral will focus on Resurrection and God's power over death.
- Presbyterians prefer that the body be present at the funeral and be buried or cremated after death. However, if cremation has occurred, the ashes should be present at the funeral.
- Interment at the cemetery will follow immediately after the funeral.
- The funeral focuses on the hope of the Resurrection, support of the bereaved, and the promise that nothing in life or death will separate the faithful from God's love.
- Flowers in the church are to be kept simple.
- Eulogies or personal remarks should be at the reception rather than at the funeral.
- The service will include a gathering, a prayer, Scriptural passages, a sermon or homily, affirmation of faith, the Lord's Prayer, a final commendation to God, and hymns. https://www.pcusa.org
- *What to do*: Visit the funeral home during scheduled visiting hours and/or attend the funeral.
- *What should you send*: Flowers, cards, donations to a charity, and food sent to the deceased's home are appropriate expressions of your sympathy.

Baptist funeral

- The pastor should be notified soon after death and will guide the bereaved through the traditions of that congregation.
- A viewing is customary either at the church or a funeral home. Most funerals occur three to five days after death.
- The deceased can be cremated or buried.
- The pastor will conduct the service, focusing on the deceased's faith life and filled with Scripture and music. The family's requests for musical favorites may be honored.

- If a eulogy is permitted at the funeral, it should also focus on faith and God's role in the deceased's life.
- Since the funeral is a religious service, it is recommended that fraternal and military honors be conducted at the viewing or the cemetery.
- It is common to have a reception after the funeral where family and friends can gather and remember the deceased.
- *What to do:* Visit the funeral home during scheduled visiting hours and/or attend the funeral.
- *What should you send:* Flowers, cards, and food to the deceased's home are appropriate expressions of your sympathy.

  https://www.everplans.com/articles/baptist-funeral-traditions https://www.yourfuneralchoice.com/attending-funeral/what-expect-baptist-funeral/

Episcopalian funeral

- The funeral liturgy is from The Book of Common Prayer. The Episcopalian practice prefers that the body be present at the funeral and cremated afterward.
- Exceptions can be made for cremation before the funeral, but the cremains should be present at the liturgy.
- The only flowers permitted in the church are those for the altar; therefore, casket sprays and other large funeral baskets are not allowed in the sanctuary during the funeral liturgy.
- Since the casket will be covered with a pall during the funeral, a casket funeral spray will not be brought into the sanctuary during the funeral.
- Episcopalians encourage donations to a charity rather than flowers.
- Music should be live either by a choir or cantor.
- Eulogies should be given at the visitation and are not considered appropriate for the funeral liturgy.
- The procession to the cemetery and burial occurs immediately after the liturgy.
- A reception follows the interment.
- *What to do:* You can pay your respects by attending the wake/viewing, if there is one, and/or the funeral.
- *What should you send:* Flowers, cards, and food to the deceased's home are appropriate expressions of your sympathy.

  https://www.everplans.com/articles/anglican-episcopalian-funeral-traditions

Roman Catholic funeral

- If a person is to be buried, a wake or viewing occurs at a funeral home or the church within 48-72 hours after death.
- A funeral liturgy typically occurs three to seven days after death at the church but may be later if cremation has been chosen.
- The family is invited to select Scripture that reflects the deceased and is invited to choose their favorite Scripturally based music for the funeral liturgy.
- Family may also participate as readers of Scripture, singers during the service.
- The only flowers permitted in the church are those for the altar; therefore, casket sprays and other large funeral baskets are not allowed in the sanctuary during the funeral liturgy.
- A funeral focuses on prayers, Scripture, songs, and the Liturgy of the Eucharist.
- The body or the cremains are often buried in a Catholic cemetery, but it is not required.
- Procession to the cemetery is an extension of the funeral liturgy and follows immediately after the funeral. Mourners may participate but are not expected to attend the burial.
- The church may provide a meal after the burial. All attendees are invited to participate.
- *Ashes may not be kept at home or scattered.* According to Catholic teaching, cremains must be interred in the earth or placed in a crypt or columbarium.
- *Note this clarification of a common misconception*: Both the *Catholic and Episcopalian faiths allow a full church funeral and burial for the victims of suicide.*
- *What to do*: You can pay your respects by attending the wake/viewing if there is one. This is a less formal gathering where you can offer condolences to the family and may be invited to speak extemporaneously. The funeral liturgy is more formal.
- *What should you send*: Floor floral arrangements are appropriate. *Floral sprays for the casket or standing arrangements may be used at the visitation*, and only one or two arrangements may be allowed in the sanctuary during the funeral. You may send food, fruit baskets, plants,

or flowers to the home. https://www.usccb.org/prayer-and-worship/sacraments-and-sacramentals/bereavement-and-funerals/overview-of-catholic-funeral-rites

Church of Jesus Christ of Latter-Day Saints (Mormon) funeral customs

- The funeral is usually held within one week of death and can take place in the place of worship, funeral home, or graveside.
- The service includes prayers and music at a church, followed by a brief service at the grave.
- The Mormon faith discourages cremation but does not forbid it.
- *What to wear*: If you attend the service, men should wear a white shirt and tie, women should wear a knee-length skirt or dress, and shoulders should be covered.
- *What should you send*: Flowers and sympathy cards are appropriate. https://www.everplans.com/articles/latter-day-saints-mormon-funeral-traditions

Islamic funeral traditions

- According to Sharia law, the body is washed and shrouded immediately after death, and the burial is performed as soon as possible.
- Since the funeral preparations must start immediately after death, there is no visitation. Mourners go to the mosque to offer prayers for the deceased.
- *What to do*: If attending the service, remember that men and women sit on separate sides of the mosque, and women must have their heads covered.
- *What should you send*: Flowers are not appropriate, but food is an acceptable expression of sympathy.
  https://www.everplans.com/articles/muslim-funeral-traditions

Hindu funeral service

- Traditionally, the body remains at the deceased's home or in a funeral home until it is cremated, usually within twenty-four hours after death. According to Hindu belief, cremation accelerates the disembodied spirit to escape from the body and obtain a new body for reincarnation.
- Black clothing is considered inappropriate; dressing in white is expected.
- There is an open casket, and guests are invited to view the body.

- The Hindu priest and senior family members conduct the ceremony. Fellow Hindus and guests of other faiths are welcome to participate but are not expected to do so.
- The body is carried to the crematorium when the viewing is over, and prayers are offered. The family remains at the crematorium until the body is fully cremated.
- Following the cremation, a period of mourning begins for thirteen to thirty days, depending on family customs.
- During this time, the family will place a photo of the deceased, often wrapped with a garland, in a place of honor for remembrance.
- *What should you send:* Flowers are appropriate for the initial service, but fruit baskets are considered the best gift to convey sympathy when visiting the home during the mourning period.
https://www.everplans.com/articles/hindu-funeral-traditions

Jewish funeral etiquette (Orthodox, Conservative, Reform)

- The body is washed immediately after death, wrapped in a white linen shroud, and placed in a closed, simple wooden casket.
- As a sign of respect, the deceased is not left alone prior to burial. Community members sit with the deceased and may recite psalms until the funeral.
- Jewish funeral services may be at the synagogue, a funeral home, or graveside.
- Readings may be in Hebrew or English.
- Before the funeral, the mourners do not mingle with the comforters.
- A rabbi is not required to conduct the funeral, but the leader must be Jewish.
- The service is solemn and is not a social gathering but may be followed by a reception at the family's home.
- **Orthodox Jews**: The deceased is buried within 24 hours of death but never on the Sabbath (Shabbat) or Jewish holidays.
- **Reformed Jews**: burial is as soon as possible, but allowances are made for travel and for the family to gather.
- It is common for several family members to participate in the burial by placing shovels of soil onto the casket.
- *What to do*: Once the body has been buried, the immediate family sits in mourning (shiva) at home for seven days. It is customary for

family, friends, and others to visit the home and offer condolences to the family. Remember that this, too, is a solemn time of mourning. The conversation should be quiet and respectful, and silence is also appropriate.

- *What should you send:* Sympathy flowers are not appropriate for a Shiva call.
- Sweet fruit, desserts, and food are appropriate gifts, but check to see if the family eats kosher (i.e., prepared in accordance with Jewish dietary guidelines) before providing any food items.

https://www.reformjudaism.org/beliefs-practices/lifecycle-rituals/death-mourning/what-expect-jewish-funeral

Buddhist funeral rites

- Buddhists believe in samsara or reincarnation.
- Many are cremated after seven days.
- There are three services: the first is held at the family home of the deceased within two to three days after death. This time permits viewing of the deceased.
- A second service is conducted five to seven days later by monks at a funeral home.
- A third and final service is held at the temple forty-nine days after the burial.
- The official mourning period ends after one hundred days.
- *What to do:* Attend the first service at the home and offer condolences to the family.
- *What should you send:* Flowers are appropriate to send to the home.
- Gourmet food gifts are *not* considered appropriate.

https://www.everplans.com/articles/buddhist-funeral-traditions/

Virtual funeral

- In 2020, during the COVID-19 pandemic, attending a loved one's funeral was impossible, so funeral homes and churches created virtual funerals for family and friends to be present at the service while not being present in the space.
- Attending a virtual funeral allows mourners to take part in a funeral from the comfort of their homes.

- For many, this new concept has become popular. Family members who are elderly, not mobile, or live miles away can attend the funeral of someone important in their lives. Ask for assistance if technology is a challenge for you.

Funeral attire

- Dress appropriately. For both men and women, business attire is your best choice.
- Although black is a traditional funeral color, attendees can wear muted dark colors or white and should dress conservatively.
- Attire for women:
    - Avoid wearing festive, casual, or bright-colored clothing.
    - Appropriate attire includes dresses (not too formal or too short), a skirt, knee length or longer, dress pants (no jeans), a top with sleeves, a blouse or a sweater.
    - Shoulders should be covered.
    - Dress shoes with modest heels or flats as you may stand for prolonged periods.
    - Jewelry should be simple and understated.
    - Avoid perfume or cologne.
    - Do not wear cocktail dresses, formal attire, or lots of glitter.

It's not about showcasing you; it is about being respectful to your loved one, friend, or colleague.

- Attire for men:
    - If you are family or a participant, you should wear a suit and tie with dress shoes.
    - Less formal attire for an attendee might include dress pants with a belt, a button-down shirt, a tie, and dress shoes.
    - Avoid wearing jeans, short-sleeved shirts, sneakers, and baseball caps.

Funeral etiquette

- Arrive at least fifteen minutes early, even if you are a guest. This time allows you to sign the guest book and possibly speak to family members.

Be sure to keep your remarks and condolences brief, as others may also be waiting to offer condolences.

- Turn your cell phone off so you will not be tempted to respond even to silenced texts. Cell phone use during a funeral or visitation is considered highly disrespectful.
- If you arrive late, do not enter the church while the family is moving. Remain in the gathering space, make your entrance inconspicuously from the side, and sit toward the back.
- Be aware that seats from the middle to the front of the service are reserved for family and close friends.
- Consider the family's background and traditions. Be sensitive to them and respond to cues from the environment.
- Send a condolence card or note after the funeral. These are important affirmations for the family.

Summary

Most funeral traditions reflect a family's culture and religious beliefs. Funerals offer us the opportunity to meet a family where they are, acknowledge their loss, experience their traditions, and join them in honoring their loved one. As our society diversifies, supporting friends and colleagues after the loss of a loved one can be intimidating, but it is an important gesture. Hopefully, you will find this information and the accompanying resources helpful.

It is important to note that as our culture continues to become increasingly more casual, funerals, like weddings, have maintained their formality. It is an important sign of respect to dress appropriately, including business rather than evening attire, and maintain proper decorum during the funeral service, which includes silencing and not looking at your cell phone.

When attending a funeral, it is important to be attentive to and respectful of the religious and cultural traditions of the family who has suffered the loss.

Chapter 14

What Is the Real Cost of Dying?

- *Your only chance to reduce the cost of a funeral at the time of death is to ask your Advocate to gather General Price Lists from funeral homes in your area before you choose one and sign a contract.*
- *This chapter aims to teach you how to read a General Price List and give you the tools to decipher it, but you can't do that unless you possess one.*
- *Price lists are updated regularly, and funeral homes state that "prices are subject to change without notice." Unfortunately, prices continue to rise annually.*

As I have stated before, funerals are one of the four most expensive purchases you will make in your lifetime. However, since they often arrive unannounced, they are likely the least researched, planned for, and budgeted large purchase you will ever make.

> ***The mission of this book is for you to consider the inevitability of death as a life event that you plan for. I am simply trying to alter our collective cultural mindset of burying our heads in the sand when it comes to death by illuminating the personal family catastrophe your procrastination may be creating.***

How often have you heard the saying, "In this world, nothing is certain except death and taxes?" Have you ever really thought about what that means? Take a moment to think about how many family deaths you have already experienced. This may vary depending on your age, but not necessarily. Family deaths are going to happen to you several times during your lifetime.

> ***Now, pause here for a moment and consider death from another angle. How many deaths could you find yourself financially responsible for, possibly a spouse, your children, your parents, or even a sibling?***

Being proactive in planning for death makes you less vulnerable not only to high funeral costs but, more importantly, to the financial fallout that you will experience in subsequent months or years. Certainly, you would shop multiple vendors for any large purchase, like an automobile or a contractor for an addition to your home. These things are in the same cost category as funerals.

Four things have been our enemy regarding planning for death

- First is our cultural unwillingness to think about death before we have to deal with it.
- Second, we don't know how expensive funerals are because discussing funeral costs is considered taboo in our society.
- Third, we don't know that we have the right to pricing information before we sign a contract.
- Fourth, we have never thought about shopping for a funeral home before we have a need; therefore, we don't have the tools to analyze costs.

I can't change the first, but I am attempting to give you the tools to accomplish challenges two through four.

As I have mentioned before, the cost of a funeral can be \$8,000–\$20,000 or more, and the cost of burial can also be an additional \$10,000–\$20,000. My research has indicated that remaining on the low end of these prices is difficult, especially if you live in a city. Let me emphasize that funeral homes and funeral directors are necessary in our society, and we need dedicated funeral directors to guide us through the process. We acknowledge that these fine people deserve to make a living, and we assume the funeral business is a business of compassion, but this is not necessarily true. The key word here is *business*.

> ***There are funeral homes in your area that prioritize compassion over profit, but you have to visit them to find out who they are.***

Like most people, you probably do not have a category in your monthly budget for a funeral. The exception is those who purchase a life insurance or burial policy and pay for it monthly or have made payments to pre-pay for a funeral. If you are older, now is an excellent time to purchase or search for a hidden or forgotten life insurance policy, an employer death benefit, or a pension benefit that may help cover funeral expenses. If you are younger, you are in an excellent position to purchase life insurance as a cushion against a tragedy and to write a will so all of your life plans can be realized for your family. Knowing whether or not you have money available is critical to making the best fiscal decisions at the time of death.

Be aware that each of the following has fees, and every:

- decision you make—to bury or cremate
- event you plan—wake, visitation, funeral, burial, or reception
- place you use—church, funeral home, or venue
- item you purchase—casket, grave liner, flowers, printed materials, or a slideshow
- service the funeral director provides—picking up your loved one from the place of death, contacting the cemetery and making burial arrangements, arranging for cremation, preparing the death certificate, use of a hearse, limousine, or a van, securing clergy, assisting with

the obituary, ordering flowers, booking police escorts, and arranging military honors for a veteran.

- person who provides a service—funeral director, staff, clergy, musicians, and even the person who digs the grave in a private cemetery *must be paid this week.*

Remember, your first connection with the funeral home is in your most vulnerable, grief-filled moment. The death has occurred only hours earlier, and whether you have expected it or not, your emotions now outrank the analytical part of your brain. The short turnaround time of a funeral and a burial creates an urgency for you to make decisions quickly. However, grief-stricken decision-makers cannot analyze prices by themselves.

The FTC says: "*Limiting the search to just one funeral home may risk paying more than necessary for the funeral or narrowing the choice of goods and services.*" Choosing a Funeral Provider | Consumer Advice (ftc.gov)

Additionally, the FTC's *Funeral Rule* requires that the funeral director present you with an invoice immediately after you make your selections to ensure you still have time to make changes before the services are rendered and the final payment is due. But are you capable of analyzing this information in real-time? This is where the counsel of your *Advocate* can be most beneficial.

It can be eye-opening to see the final invoice, especially if you have not consciously questioned the price of each suggested item. Think of your bill as a rolling tally, like a gas pump. Every time you nod and passively accept another item or service from the funeral director, you may add hundreds or even thousands of dollars to your final invoice, so this is an important time to have someone else looking after your bottom line.

The critical takeaway is that for a burial, you need a casket, a grave liner, a cemetery plot, and some flowers, but you may not know the wide range of prices for these items and other goods or services offered by a funeral home. Before a sudden death, you may not have considered cremation and might not be aware that this may be a less costly option.

Additionally, you can only monitor costs if you first have considered what is important to you and understand how to compare prices. Unfortunately, late in my research, I discovered that many funeral services come layered with fees that can take an accountant's eye to decipher. More than one funeral director, in violation of the *Funeral Rule*, condescendingly told me, " If you insist, I will give you a copy of the price list but understand that these price lists are complicated and difficult to understand. Please call *when* you have questions."

So, I ask you, do you think you will be able to compare prices and discover hidden fees if:

- you have just suffered a loss?
- you are unaware you have the "right" to see all price lists?
- the price list seems complicated?

Having facts available up front may take some of the emotion and confusion from the decision-making process. For instance, as discussed in *Chapter* 6, you should receive a *Casket Price List* with the cost of each casket the funeral home sells before they show any of them to you. Marketing research indicates that you will purchase one of the first three caskets you see. So, you will likely be shown the most expensive caskets first, and you may have to ask to see cheaper ones, which may be in a utility room or warehouse. Recording your findings from price lists using the **Funeral Home Price Comparison Worksheet** in *Appendix* B will give you a clear picture of the funeral homes in your area.

Throughout this book, I have made general statements about the industry and its pricing practices. In this chapter, I will give the numbers verifying those statements. I encourage you to take a few hours to gather pricing information in your area before you need it.

In this chapter, I will share 2024 prices from around the country. I will compare urban and rural prices alongside the median prices of the *National Funeral Directors Association* (NFDA 2021 *numbers*).

Pricing for a funeral with burial

This chart provides a comparison of prices in three categories:

1. A range of costs for a funeral with burial in a large urban area.
2. The *National Funeral Director's Association*'s—one size fits all—cost of funerals for anywhere in the country.
3. A range of funeral and burial costs in rural areas of the country.

Each funeral home must provide three price lists:

1. Items and services required for a funeral — *General Price List.*
2. Prices for caskets and urns — *Casket Price List.*
3. Prices for burial containers such as grave liners and vaults, markers, and monuments — *Burial Container Price List.*

Chart 1—Funeral with Burial— *General Price List*

The chart below will familiarize you with the items found on a *General Price List* (GPL) as required by the Federal Trade Commission's *Funeral Rule.* The FTC requires that the services listed in BOLD be on every GPL in the U.S. Each line item describes goods and services you may need for your funeral with a burial.

General Price List — Funeral with Burial

General Price List	Urban Area	NFDA	Rural Area
Basic Services Fee	$2,600–$5,700	$2,300	$1,800–$3,000
Embalming *(required for a viewing)*	$950-$1,600	$775	$200–$500
Refrigeration per day	$300-$500	-	$50–$150
Other Body Preparations	$725-$950	-	$200–$1,080
Dressing, cosmetic enhancement	$450–$1,600	$275	$175–$300
Special care for autopsied bodies	$150–$500	-	$350

Facilities Use and Staff

	Urban Area	NFDA	Rural Area
Facilities and staff for a viewing	$700–$800	$450	$300–$1,195
Funeral home use - staff for funeral	$800–$1,600	$515	$475-$995
Graveside service with staff facilitating	$700–$1,300	–	$225-$895
Overseeing interment of an urn	$350	–	$350
Transportation	**Urban Area**	**NFDA**	**Rural Area**
Transfer from place of death to funeral home	$1,100	$350	$300-$850
Transfer to and from the airport	$250–$500	–	$350
Transfer from funeral home to place of autopsy	$250–$600	–	$300
Transfer to and from the crematory	$300	–	–
Use of hearse	$550–$950	$350	$300–$500
Use of limousine	$500	–	$160–$500
Use of service vehicle	$300	$150	$90
Transportation outside of radius of the funeral home	$3.00–$5.00/ mile	–	$2.80–$4.00/mile
Forwarding remains to another funeral home	$4,200–$5,940	–	$2,400–$3,900
Receiving remains from an airport to the cemetery, crematory, or other funeral home	$2,900–$4,460	–	$2,400–$2,800
Direct Cremation			
Transfer of remains, crematory fee, *Basic Services Fee*–without a visitation or funeral	$2,400–$3,550	$2,183	$1,700–$3,795
Cost of an alternative container	$200–$5,000	–	Included
Immediate Burial			
Transfer of remains–*Basic Services Fee*–without a visitation or funeral—No casket	$4,450–$6,900	$2,597	$1,700–$4,390
Basic casket	$2,000	–	$2,000

General **Price List–Cash Advance Purchases**	**Urban Area**	**NFDA**	**Rural Area**
Guest book	$50–$110	*Package* $183	$60.00
Prayer cards (100)	$60–$100	-	$135
Thank you, cards (25)	$30	-	$12.50
Musicians/vocalist/ accompanist honorarium	$300–$500	-	$150–$300
Clergy honorarium	$300–$700	-	$150
Mailing of cremated remains—DIY—USPS— $30	$125	-	$175
Caskets	$1,100–$11,300	-	$1,600–$2,375
Stained hardwood	$2,300–$4,200	$1,300-$1,500	$2,400
Solid oak	$4,200	-	$2,450
Solid cherry	$5,500–$6,700	$2,000	$2,980
Solid mahogany	$8,000	$2,900	$3,600
Wood veneer	-	$1,300–$1,500	$1,995
18-gauge steel	$3,600–$4,200	$1,100	$1,795
Rental Casket	$1,000–$1,600	$995	$995
Rental casket insert	$300	-	$300
Urns	$100–$1,300	$120–$300	$185–$1385
Outer Burial Containers	$1,600–$5,600	$1,572	$1,450–$6,100

Cemetery Costs

Cemetery Expenses	**Urban Area**	**NFDA**	**Rural Area**
Cemetery Fees– opening and closing fees	$1,000–$5,000	-	$200–$500
Interment—adult—casket	$2,200	$1000–$3,000	$500
Burial of an urn—adult	$1,300	-	$350
Placement of an urn in a niche	$1,000	-	-
Weekend, after-hours, or holiday burials	$500–$1,200	-	$1,100
Processing fees	$50–$400	-	-
Outer Burial Containers	$1,600–$5,600	$1,572	$1,825

Burial Vaults

	Urban Area	NFDA	Rural Area
For urns	$700–$1,400	–	$250–$565
For caskets	$1,600–$5,600	–	$1,100–$3,200
Grave Liner for a casket	$1,400–$3,200	$1,572	$1,572
Interment Options			
Burial plots	$3,500–$12,000	$2000–$5,000	$500
Mausoleum	$6,400–$19,000	–	–
Exterior niche marble-granite	$400–$5,000	–	–
Columbarium	$6,500	–	–
Plot for urns	$200–$6,5000	–	$500
Multiple urns 2-6	$11,000–$35,000	–	$500

Observations about NFDA prices

The chart above comparing rural, urban, and NFDA pricing is enlightening. Notice that the NFDA's *median* prices are closest to rural pricing and are at the bottom of the range for an urban area. If these items are necessary and charged by a funeral home, then the NFDA prices are unrealistic, especially in cities. This may be due to the fact that the NFDA chose to use *median* prices rather than *mean* or *average* prices in the information they release to the public. This choice seems to have skewed the price data dramatically, possibly due to the size and parameters of the sample toward significantly deflated lower costs. And yet, I have seen these NFDA prices for both a funeral with burial and a cremation quoted on almost every internet search I conducted. They are cited by journalists, bloggers, and businesses online. They are quoted by financial planners, insurance companies, estate attorneys, online funeral businesses, and any website that deals with funeral goods or planning. In short, the NFDA is the "go-to" reference for anyone citing funeral pricing, but are they a reliable source for pricing in *your* area? Don't assume the *median* national price will be accurate for you, and the only way for you to know is to visit funeral homes and secure *General Price Lists.*

> ***You will be one of the wise ones if you do not accept this second-hand information on funeral pricing. It is best to do your own research and gather GPLs from your local funeral homes to assess how much funeral expenses will realistically cost in your community.***

Chart 2—Funeral home price comparisons for a funeral with a burial

The chart below lists one corporate and three private funeral homes within an eight-mile radius of each other that serve the same area in a major city suburb. It lists the itemized prices of necessary funeral goods and services. Notice the significant price differences among businesses that compete for the same market share. This is proof that visiting three or four funeral homes in your area and filling out the **Funeral Home Price Comparison Worksheet** may be worth your time.

Funeral with Burial	**Funeral Home 1**	**Funeral Home 2**	**Funeral Home 3**	**Funeral Home 4**
Basic Services Fee	$5,650	$2,600	$3,750	$4,800
Embalming	$1,600	$950	$1,275	$1,400
Casketing	$400	$225	$350	$175
Staff for visitation	$700	$800	$700	$700
Staff for a funeral at FH	$1,600	$800	$850	$1,000
Staff for funeral- church	$1,600	$800	$700	$1,500
Pick-up-place of death	$1,100	$600	$825	$1,300
Funeral vehicle/hearse	$500	$950	$675	$500
Utility vehicle-flowers	$300	$400	$275	$225
Limousine -3 hours	$500	$500	$500	$675
Printed materials	$110	$210	$110	$95
Casket-least expensive	$2,500	$2,000	$2,000	$2,200
Refrigeration per day	$500	$310	$375	$400
Staff for cemetery	$1,300	$700	$600	$1,100
Grave liner	$1,600	$950	$1,200	Not listed
Burial vault	$1,500	$1,550	$1,200	Not listed
Insurance processing fee	Not listed	3.9%	5%	Not listed
Police escort	$600	$600	$600	$675
Rental casket + insert	$1,300	Not listed	$1,225	Not listed

Price comparisons for cremation

> ***Walking into a funeral home and saying that you want to have your loved one cremated is not as straightforward as you might think. I thought that you only had to make that one decision and the rest would take care of itself—that is, until I started collecting and analyzing price lists. Some funeral directors seem to have created many nuanced ways of providing —or should I say—selling cremation.***

Here is one rural private funeral home's simple, straightforward description with a reasonable price. *If it only could be this simple for everyone— everywhere!*

Direct Cremation (no viewing or ceremony)

• Limited services of funeral director and staff	$900
• Transfer of remains to funeral home	$300
• Sanitary care of remains	$200
• Cremation fee	$300
• Alternative container for cremation	$100
• **Total**	**$1,800**

Option 1: *Direct Cremation* using a funeral home—the fine print matters.

Direct Cremation is one of the first options you see on a GPL. One would think it would be straightforward, but further analysis is necessary. If you carefully read the fine print below the words *Direct Cremation*, you may discover items that have been left out but are needed—notably a cremation container to transfer the body to the crematory. Several different containers were available, and they increased the charge for *Direct Cremation* by $175–$450.

Another item I questioned was the statement, "Transfer to OR from the crematory." Upon further investigation, I discovered that the charge for transportation to OR from the crematory was $295. Is this a "hidden fee?" Since I do not plan to drive myself to the crematory, could my family be charged an extra $295 to retrieve my cremains?

These carefully crafted omissions lead to misleading pricing for the average customer and illustrate that the fine print really does matter. However, the funeral home covers itself with the following FTC wording that appears at the top of every price list I collected.

> **The FTC says**: "*The goods and services shown below are those we can provide to our customers. You may choose only the items you desire. However, any funeral arrangements you select will include a charge for our basic services and overhead. If legal or other requirements mean you must buy any items you did not specifically ask for, we will explain the reason in writing on the statement we provide describing the funeral goods and services you selected.*"
> https://www.ftc.gov/business-guidance/resources/complying-funeral-rule#the-general-price-list

In another case, a private rural funeral home posted its *Direct Cremation* price as $3,300. It clearly stated that this fee did not include the crematory fee, which, by the way, was not included anywhere on their price list. I found the regional crematory fee of $445 on a separate document from a competitor, but I have no idea what this business charges its customers— or will they— until they see their invoice. In addition, this business added the following quote from the FTC to its GPL:

> **The FTC says:** "*This list does not include prices for certain items that you may ask us to buy for you, such as cemetery or crematory services, flowers, and newspaper notices. The prices for those items will be shown on your bill or the statement describing the funeral goods and services you selected.*"

Bingo! They admitted there is a hidden fee and gave themselves permission to collect it! There is something inherently wrong about purchasing a *Direct Cremation* package that does not include the cremation or the crematory fee, but what grieving family would figure this out beforehand? They would likely shake their head and pay the bill.

What is really included in your *Direct Cremation* package? You will only know for sure if you read the fine print.

The following chart analyzes the content of the *fine print* description under the heading *Direct Cremation* on the GPL of four funeral homes. The check marks indicate what is included under that heading. By filling out this chart with prices from your local funeral homes, you will be able to see which items are included and which may have been omitted and may require an additional fee.

Chart 3—Price comparisons for *Direct Cremation* at four funeral homes in the same urban area.

What is included?	**Funeral Home 1**	**Funeral Home 2**	**Funeral Home 3**	**Funeral Home 4**
GPL price of Cremation	**$2,385**	**$2,400**	**$2,800**	**$3,795**
"*Basic Services Fee*"	✓	✓	✓	✓
Transfer of remains	✓	✓	✓	✓
Preparation of remains	–	✓	✓	✓
Death certificate & permits	✓	✓	✓	✓
Refrigeration	✓	✓	✓	✓
Transfer to crematory	✓	✓	✓	✓
Crematory fee	✓	✓	$295	✓
Alternate cremation container	$175–$450	–	✓	✓
Basic urn included	–	–	✓	✓
Items below this line are added to the price on the GPL				
Visitation for family 15 min	$495	–	–	*30 min included*
Mail cremains for you	$135	$300-$500	$135	$85
Mail cremains yourself USPS	**$30**	**$30**	**$30**	**$30**
Witness the cremation	–	–	$495	$250
Urn (*various prices*)	–	–	–	–
Total	**$2,560–$2,880**	**$2,400**	**$3,095**	**$3,795**

Chart 4—Price comparisons for *Direct Cremation* for four family-owned funeral homes in the same urban area.

Family owned	Funeral Home 1	Funeral Home 2	Funeral Home 3	Funeral Home 4
Direct Cremation	**$4,310**	**$2,400**	**$2,790**	**$1,695**
Price for a container	$595	Included	Included	Included
Total	**$4,905**	**$2,400**	**$2,970**	**$1,695**

Can you now see how doing this exercise proves that price differences are significant and may make your decision crystal clear? But once again, I ask, how likely are you to perform this exercise if you have just suffered a loss?

Observation: After studying these price lists, I found that a low-price *Direct Cremation* from a *privately owned funeral home* was less costly in all but one case. The price chart above seems simple, but somehow, in the table below, it got complicated, *or maybe it just needed to be more profitable.*

Below are price comparisons for *Direct Cremation* at four funeral homes using *Trayview* containers. The description of the container is as follows: "*Direct Cremation* with Trayview container—a *cardboard* exterior and a *crepe paper* mattress and pillow. Note: *Funeral homes 2-4 are within an eight-mile radius of each other.*

Chart 5—Price comparisons for a Direct Cremation with the cremation container omitted and then listed separately.

	Funeral Home 1	Funeral Home 2	Funeral Home 3	Funeral Home 4
Price for Direct Cremation	**$3,545**	**$1,965**	**$2,385**	**$3,785**
Price for *Trayview* container	$395	$395	$395	$395
Total	**$3,940**	**$2,360**	**$2,780**	**$4,180**

The *Direct Cremation* price is what you will be quoted if you call for a price over the phone or if you verbally ask a funeral director for their price for cremation and do not see a price list. The container cost may be the *surprise* cost that will show up later on your invoice. As stated earlier, the funeral home is legally covered by using the FTC disclaimer above regarding adding items to your invoice. *Note that the FTC crafted the wording.*

Each of these funeral homes offers five choices for cremation containers. In addition, Funeral Home 1 would also like to provide you with a mahogany casket for $14,140 to go up in smoke, bringing your *less expensive Direct Cremation* to $17,585 with *no viewing* and *no funeral* service. But I pose this question:

> ***If you do not pay extra to witness the cremation, how do you know that they do not use a cardboard container rather than your mahogany casket at the time of cremation?***

I suspect that others may have thought of this, leading funeral homes to charge an additional fee for attending a cremation.

In addition, *Direct Cremation* offerings indicate that there is no special interior for two of the containers offered, but in a separate section of the price list under "Alternative Containers," you can purchase an ivory crepe interior with a pillow for $95. This would make the least expensive container listed at $175 now cost $270, all because you agreed that you wanted your deceased loved one to be more comfortable on the way to the crematorium. This is an example of how a simple nod of your head during your fog of grief can trigger what I call a *less-than-transparent fee.*

But the real question is, how do you feel about paying $175 to $450 for a box made of cardboard, laminated wood, or fiberboard that you will never see and will be consumed during cremation? One of my internet searches indicated that the wholesale cost of a suitable functional cardboard container could cost the funeral home as little as $12.50.

Chart 6— Cremation using a funeral home vs. a direct cremation facility.

Now let's compare a *Direct Cremation* using a funeral home vs. a direct cremation facility.

Direct *Cremation*—Funeral Home		**Direct Cremation Facility**	
Basic Services Fee, transfer of remains from a local place of death to the funeral home, refrigeration, crematory fee, death certificates, no visitation by family	*$3,800	*Basic Services Fee*, transfer of remains from a local place of death to the funeral home, refrigeration, crematory fee, death certificates, no visitation by family cremation container decorative urn/box	$2,800 OR if you choose the package that returns your body home from anywhere in the country or the world $3,500
Cremation container	$1,095	Included	Included
Pine container	$450		
Fiberboard container	$395		
Trayview container	*$175		
Cardboard container			
Urn	*$250	Included	Decorative box included
Funeral home price	**TOTAL** ***$4,225**	**Direct Cremation Facility**	**Total** **$2,800**

As you can see, these prices can be comparable if you insist on the least expensive container option and don't buy the interior container package. Also, be sure there is no additional fee for returning the cremains to you.

One of the best prices for a basic cremation is with a national corporate-owned cremation business, which includes the cost of the cremation container for $2,800 (2024).

Their basic services include:

- picking up the deceased at the place of death.
- collecting basic information for filing the death certificate.
- signing forms and permissions.
- taking the body to the crematory.
- returning the ashes to the family.
- including a decorative box for ashes.

It should also be noted that the cost of the cremation container and the crematory fee are included. However, if you live in a rural area, check your local prices for *Direct Cremation* and then determine if a national cremation business like the Neptune Society, National Cremation, or Trident Society are available to you.

The best price for cremation in my city is with a private crematory: $800. This includes the transfer of your loved one to their facility, the cremation, filing necessary permits, and providing one copy of the death certificate, with curbside pickup of the cremains in a temporary container. In the end, I actually purchased a direct cremation from a private funeral home in my city for $1,950 because I interviewed the funeral director and was impressed with a funeral service they provided a friend.

Chart 7— Some corporate funeral homes offer several cremation packages.

All prices in this chart are found on the same *General Price List*. Note: **Package 1** is a funeral with a visitation with the body present using a rental casket with cremation to follow. **Packages 2** and **3** are cremation-only but with different items listed, and the final column is the price listed under the mandatory heading— *Direct Cremation.*

By filling out this same chart yourself with funeral homes in your area using the **Funeral Home Price Comparison Worksheet** in *Appendix* B, it quickly becomes clear which services you receive for the listed prices.

Cremation Packages	**Funeral + Cremation**	**Package 2**	**Package 3**	**Direct Cremation**
Basic Services Fee	✓	✓	✓	✓
Refrigeration	✓	✓	✓	✓
Transfer of remains to funeral home	✓	✓	✓	✓
Transfer to or from the crematory	✓	✓	✓	✓
Crematory fee	✓	✓	✓	✓
Printed memorial package	✓	✓	-	-
Guest Book	✓	-	-	-
Internet memorial	✓	✓	-	-
Flowers	✓	✓	-	-
Urn	✓	✓	✓	-
Reception value $1,300-$1,500	✓	✓	-	-
Trayview cremation container	-	✓	✓	$395
Funeral Service	✓	✓	-	-

Burial Package	Package 1	Package 2	Package 3	Direct Cremation
Embalming	✓	NA	NA	NA
Dressing casketing	✓	NA	NA	NA
Visitation	✓	NA	NA	NA
Limousine	✓	NA	NA	NA
Rental casket	✓	NA	NA	NA
Rental casket insert	✓	NA	NA	NA
Not Included				
Cremation container	$175–$450	NA	NA	$175–$450
Return of ashes from the crematorium?	$295?	$295?	$295?	$295?
See the chart below for a comparison of the final prices				

Chart 8—Cremation Packages—the real prices

Using the package prices listed above, the chart below compares the prices for each of the three packages plus *Direct Cremation* at four different funeral homes in the same service area. The items listed above as "Not Included" have *not* been added to the total prices. However, you may be required to purchase them.

Listed Price	Package 1	Package 2	Package 3	Direct Cremation
Funeral Home 1	$17,000	$7,000	$3,300	$2,800
Funeral Home 2	$11,000	$5,400	$2,800	$2,400
Funeral Home 3	$15,000	$8,000	$4,600	$4,200
Funeral Home 4	$16,100	$15,600	$8,900	$4,800

This chart lists the range of prices of three funeral homes within an thirty-mile radius of each other in an urban area. It should convince you how different prices can be among competitors and *how critical it is for you to shop around and plan ahead.* These are substantial amounts of money.

Take a moment to consider how a death could impact your budget, your future debt, or your savings.

Package Prices

Typically, the purpose of a package is to bundle commonly purchased items together and present them at a price less than if the items were purchased separately. For people who are distraught, a package should ideally reduce the number of decisions they must make. It should be a win-win for both parties—*that is, if the package contains all of the items that the purchaser needs and nothing extra.* I did not find this to be the case.

> *The FTC says: "Many funeral homes offer package funerals that may cost less than buying individual items or services.* ***Offering package funerals is permitted by law as long as an itemized price list is also provided. But you can't accurately compare total costs unless you use the price lists."*** https://consumer.ftc.gov/articles/choosing-funeral-provider

---

What to look for in package pricing to determine if it is the best option for you.

> ***You can't accurately compare a "package price" for a cremation or a funeral with a burial unless you have a General Price List in your hand.***

Step 1: Here are the items you can expect to see on a General Price List for cremation:

- *Basic Services Fee*
- Transfer from place of death
    - Death certificate and permits
    - Refrigeration
    - Transfer of the body to the crematory
    - Cremation container
    - Cremation fee
    - Return of the cremains to you.
    - Additional crematory fee? *This fee is sometimes omitted and added later.*
    - Urn vs. basic cardboard or plastic container
    - Fee to witness the cremation *(optional)*

Step 2: Using the *General Price List*, make a list of the items included in the fine print of the package you are considering.

- Are all of the items you need from the list above included in the package?
- If not, make a note of the missing items, then, using the GPL, determine how much each item costs.
- Common missing items may include:
  - an alternative container—for transporting remains
  - return of the cremains to you
  - crematory use fee
  - cremation fee

- Now, carefully read the fine print. Is there anything in the fine print that you do not want? Common items include:
  - an overpriced container or burial casket
  - embalming
  - a reception

- Using the GPL, identify the cost of the item(s) you do not wish to use.
- Examine the fine print and determine if those items can be credited back to you or exchanged for another item.

Here's what I discovered about the *fine print.* This statement is listed below each package on the General Price List of some of the funeral homes I visited.

If a consumer chooses not to use any good or service included in a package, at the time of purchase, no credit or refund will be issued.

The actual font size on the price list is shown below.

If a consumer chooses not to use any good or service included in a package, at the time of purchase, no credit or refund will be issued.

If you had just been notified of a death, would you have read the fine print when you chose your funeral package plan? You definitely could not have read it without seeing the *General Price List* that stated it.

> ***It is more common than you might think not to receive a General Price List at the time of purchase. However, it is important to understand that whether you see the GPL or not, once you sign a contract with that funeral home, you are still bound to all of the policies within.***

Step 3: Do the following to determine if purchasing a package is beneficial for you

- Compare the prices of the items on your list to the package list to see if *items you need are missing* or *items you don't need are included* in the package. Use the **Funeral Home Price Comparison Worksheet** provided in *Appendix* B to make this easier to do.
- Accept a package price only if it includes everything you need for the cremation or burial and nothing else.
- Remember, as stated above, in almost all cases, there are no substitutions in a package, and no credit will be given if items in the package are left unused.
- Prior to confirming your selection, ask the funeral director if any additional items might be required for the funeral or cremation, which will incur additional charges to the package price.

Before you commit to a package, insist that the funeral director present you with a sample final invoice guaranteeing that no additional items will be required—thus affirming that the price listed is the FINAL price!

FOR ADDITIONAL PROTECTION, consider asking the funeral director to sign your invoice, guaranteeing what you are seeing is your final price!

Buyer beware! Why are all of these steps necessary?

Burial and cremation packages can be a way for funeral directors to:

- Omit items you need, thus requiring you to purchase them in addition to the cost of the package.
- Insert items such as a reception that you do not want or will not use while still requiring you to pay for them.
- Omit and add items, thus inflating the actual cost of the package up to—or above—the cost of the itemized options.

This is a classic *bait-and-switch* tactic.

- You are convinced psychologically that the package price is less expensive.

- After committing to the package, you are informed that you will need to purchase another item.
- You ask if you can exchange an item you need for one that you do not intend to use.
- You are told that this is not possible according to company policy.

Here is what could happen if you purchase a funeral or cremation package but never see a *General Price List*.

- You might be given a verbal price for the package or a written summary of charges by the funeral director without ever being shown a *General Price List*.
- You would have found missing items like a burial container, the presence of the staff at the cemetery, the fee for the crematory, or an alternative cremation container on your invoice.
- You may have learned that your package contained a reception valued at $1,000 or more but chose not to use it because people at your house of worship were planning a reception for you at no charge.
- You might ask to exchange the reception for one of the missing items.
- The funeral director will apologetically refuse, stating it is against company policy.
- You might decide to protest your final invoice.
- The funeral director would *then* show you the *General Price List* to prove that they had the right to enforce their policy.
- Of course, you were unaware of their policy because you had never seen a *General Price List*.
- This is a circular argument that you will always lose.
- I ask realistically, what will you do—take them to court or pay the bill?

Is it possible to control the cost of a funeral?

Yes, it is. Remember, you need a funeral director to transfer the remains from the place of death, secure permits, file the death certificate, and maintain custody of the body until it is interred. *You do not have to use their services to plan a funeral* if you plan an *Immediate Burial* or a *Direct Cremation*. Once the remains are cremated or buried, you can use the CHECKLIST in *Chapter* 5 to plan a memorial service or celebration of life immediately after death or sometime in the future at a place of your choosing.

Money-saving options for a funeral and burial:

- Consider an *Immediate Burial* as listed on any GPL.
- Choose an inexpensive casket, possibly one made of pine.
- Contract directly with the cemetery.
- Plan the funeral yourself using the CHECKLIST in *Chapter* 5.

Money-saving options for cremation at a direct cremation facility—least expensive

The following items should be included:

- *Basic Services Fee* for funeral director and staff
- Transfer of remains from the place of death to the crematory
- Permits and filing of the death certificate
- Crematory fee
- Refrigeration
- Transfer to and from the crematory
- The cost of the cremation
- Cardboard cremation container
- Return of cremains to your family

Direct Cremation through a reputable funeral home that does not play pricing games. Be sure you know what is included and what is not included. Here is the list you need to make your assessment:

- *Basic Services Fee* for funeral director and staff
- Transfer of remains from place of death
- Permits and filing the death certificate
- Crematory fee
- Refrigeration
- Transfer to and from the crematory
- Cremation
- Return of cremains to your family
- Be sure to determine the cost of an alternative container before signing a contract. It should not exceed $300. If it does, check out the other options listed in this chapter.

Other ways to save money

- After *Direct Cremation* or *Immediate Burial*, use the information in *Chapter* 5 to plan a funeral without a funeral director.
- Contact your house of worship. They may provide a memorial service and a reception at a reduced cost or possibly for a donation if you are a member.

Pre-planning—not necessarily pre-paying—is your best option

- Pre-pay for cremation or burial if death is anticipated due to age or illness. Pre-need prices can be up to 20% lower than at the time of service.
- Visit local funeral homes to obtain your location's price lists (GPLs). Use the **Funeral Home Price Comparison Worksheet** provided in *Appendix* B to make price comparisons so you can determine your best options.

At the time of death

- Begin by gathering at least three price lists in your area.
- Take your time, especially if you have family travel needs to accommodate. Remember, planning a funeral in three to seven days is no longer necessary unless you want a visitation and burial. However, you may have to consider the cost of refrigeration.
- Choose only the services you need.
- Ask your *Advocate* to gather price lists, compare them on the **Funeral Home Price Comparison Worksheet** in *Appendix* B, and monitor costs constantly. Advise them to look for hidden fees at the time of death.
- Resist upselling by the funeral director, cemetery personnel, or other vendors.
- Choose budget-friendly options for:
    - Casket or urn—purchase online.
    - Facility usage—find a low-cost or rent-free facility for the funeral.
    - Flowers—one or two simple or self-made arrangements.
    - Printed materials—print your own.
    - Transportation—use family or friend's cars.
    - Reception—celebrate at someone's home or in a park.

- Interment—delay or eliminate by cremating. In this case, keeping your loved one's ashes at home or scattering them are two cost-free options.

If all of this seems overwhelming to you, consider donating your loved one's body to a *reputable* medical school, university, or research facility.

There may be fees associated with donation. It is best to consider universities and medical schools in your area and call them directly for details.

If you are considering other non-university options, be sure to read this disturbing article regarding how some donation organizations treat and broker bodies. https://www.reuters.com/investigates/special-report/usa-bodies-brokers/

Good news and bad news

The good news:

- If you look carefully at the two cremation charts listed in this chapter, you can see cremation prices ranging from $2,780 to about $5,000.
- If you look carefully and plan ahead, you may be able to have your loved one cremated for under $3,000 if you limit the services of a funeral home to cremation only and you plan your own funeral.
- Part two of the good news is that if you plan ahead, you can pay for these services monthly, possibly with your local funeral home or a direct cremation facility.
- You can also lock in your price at today's rates.
- If you live in a major city, you may have access to a wholesale cremation-only facility for about $1,000.
- Here's the best news of all. If you purchase a life insurance policy especially if you are young, you can make sure that not only funeral expenses will be paid for, but possibly even your home and your children's education will be funded as well.

The bad news:

- Even the least expensive, carefully researched, and pre-planned after-death care will cost you a minimum of $3,000.

- Could you pay that amount next week without taking out a loan or creating credit card debt?

Summary

I obtained pricelists from around the country not only through my travels but also with the help of my friends and their relatives. There is a lot to digest here, but it substantiates the need for comparative pricing, as illustrated in this chapter.

As you read this book, you are becoming aware that death has become very expensive and complicated, especially if you live in a city. The cultural norm of refusing to think about or discuss death before it is a reality only makes things worse and can put your family in financial jeopardy if your number comes up in the death lottery.

Funeral directors seem quite confident of five things at the time of your family death:

1. You will never ask for, read, or analyze their *General Price List*.
2. You won't question or challenge their prices.
3. You will sign their contract in stunned silence.
4. When you get the final invoice, you will pay whatever they charge according to the terms of their policy, whether you can afford it or not.
5. You will say nothing regarding the cost of the funeral to anyone in the coming weeks or months, either out of shock for the money you've spent or out of respect for your loved one, as you make payments for months or years to come.

Many people are completely unaware of the tempest that will strike at the end of their life or that of a loved one. My intention throughout the book has been to sound the alarm and give you tools to help you plan and protect your loved ones. Let's spread the word, beginning with your family!

Chapter 15

How Are We Going to Pay for This?

- *Let's go back to the original question—could you write a check to a funeral home and cemetery for $8,000–$20,000 next week?*
- *Would an expense this large cause you to take on more debt?*
- *Over 42% of Americans do not have enough savings to cover an unexpected expense of $1,000 for a car repair or emergency room visit.*
- *Only 11% of the 330 million people in the U.S. have $25,000 in savings—and what if the cost of a funeral depletes your entire nest egg?*

You're not alone if the funeral pricing listed in the previous chapter seems overwhelming. It very well may be that way for most of the U.S. population. In fact, in 2022, nearly 63%, or 125 million people, lived paycheck to paycheck, according to CNBC. The definition of living paycheck to paycheck means that you can manage your monthly bills, but nothing is left over. Unfortunately, the cost of a funeral and burial may cause you to lose your financial stability. Not only is the average price of a funeral $8,000 or more, but for many people this expense arrives unannounced and unexpected.

As I have stated previously, *the funeral home and cemetery require full payment before your loved one is cremated or buried*, so once a death occurs, someone is responsible for this debt within a week!

> ***Funeral expenses are neither a purchase you can decline to make nor a debt you can refuse to pay.***

Can you or your family members be forced to pay for a funeral?

The answer is yes and no. After a death, you have no choice but to employ a funeral director for the disposition of a body. So, the short answer is that *someone* must pay for a cremation or burial once a death has occurred. This is why it is essential to have a plan for paying funeral costs before signing a contract and, ideally, before a death.

> ***The only person legally required to pay for the funeral is the person who signs the contract with the funeral home.***

In the case of a parent or sibling's death, when there is little or no money in the estate to pay final expenses, your family may be eager to help financially at the time of death. However, as the reality of the expense sets in, they may choose not to honor their commitment. It is prudent for the person who signs the contract with the funeral home to have other significant family members sign a written agreement stating that they are all assuming this expense jointly. Creating a document that all parties sign gives the benefactor more security for repayment in this agreement.

Conversely, not having a formal agreement can lead to permanent fractures in these relationships.

> ***The only way to pay for a funeral in installments is to pre-pay before death or purchase an insurance policy for that purpose.***

You know money is available in your loved one's accounts; how do you legally access it?

Unfortunately, the short answer is most likely you can't. If the deceased's accounts do not have *payable-on-death* or other beneficiary designations or there are no *joint accounts established before death*, you most likely cannot access this money. These funds will not be available until the probate court releases them, and that will be months from now or longer.

The first places to look for money

- Look for insurance policies and check the death benefit.
- Some employers provide insurance with a death benefit for their employees or offer insurance policies that employees can purchase. Check with the employer's HR department.
- Some pension plans for seniors contain a death benefit, especially if your loved one worked for a large corporation or a state or federal government.
- Note that Social Security only pays a $255 death benefit.
- Check if bank accounts have beneficiaries. Note that *payable-on-death* (POD) beneficiary designations are what the name indicates. The money in this account is available to the beneficiaries named on the account when a death certificate is presented to the financial institution. This money is not included in the estate and does not have to go through probate. *However, assign these designations with caution, as the beneficiaries have no obligation to pay your final expenses once the money is released.*
- Also, check if investment accounts have beneficiary designations.
- If your loved one is or was a trade union member, look for documents associated with membership. You may find an insurance policy there.

Ethnic or religious fraternal orders have special rates on insurance policies. Here are the ten most popular organizations in the U.S. If your loved one was a member, there may be a policy you don't know about:

- Veterans of Foreign Wars (VFW)
- American Legion
- Knights of Columbus
- Rotary Club
- Loyal Order of Moose
- The Independent Order of Odd Fellows
- The Benevolent and Protective Order of Elks
- Masonic Lodges
- Order of Sons of Italy in America
- Fraternal Order of Eagles

Medicaid

Medicaid is a federal government insurance program that assists individuals who do not have the resources to pay for health care. Some funeral assistance may be available if your loved one was on Medicaid. Since these programs are state administered, search your state's website for their terms of Medicaid funeral expenses.

Publish and share your need for funding on your social media platform.

Family, friends, coworkers, members of your church or social group, and even strangers may donate to your fund. Many people find it difficult to solicit funds from friends and strangers, but think of it this way: You will simply state your need, and it will be each donor's choice to give, which may provide you with valuable financial relief.

Crowdfunding

Crowdfunding allows you to set up a campaign for your loved one's funeral expenses. It may feel uncomfortable to ask for money, but everyone knows how expensive funerals can be. You can raise money quickly to move forward in planning your funeral. Consider asking for donations to your fund instead of flowers.

How do I set up a funding request?

- Choose a platform like—EverLoved—GoFundMe, or other crowdsourcing websites.
- Set up an account.
- Tell your story.
- List your financial goal based on your expenses.
- Request donations.
- Share with your friends via email and social media.

Websites dedicated to funeral fundraising:

Fund the Funeral— www.fundthefuneral.com

Be sure to check out this website. This fund has established a fraud-free crowdfunding platform devoted to helping people with final expenses. The fund's founder, Jonathan Fisher, a funeral director, saw firsthand the devastating effect funeral expenses had on families. The fund's fees are small and used for website maintenance. Donations are paid directly to the funeral home via an electronic transfer to prevent fraud. This platform is open to families whose only option is crowdfunding.

Ever Loved— www.everloved.com

Registering with everloved.com, you can search funeral homes in your area, compare prices, and read reviews for each. You can see itemized prices for each service you need for burial or cremation and other funeral items like caskets, urns, grave liners, and markers.

The platform allows you to:

- create a free personalized website for your loved one.
- find a template to write an obituary and post it for free.
- share information about funeral events—dates, times, places.
- set up a fundraiser for friends and the community to contribute to your funeral expenses.
- find caskets, urns, and other funeral products.
- add your favorite charity.
- send thank you notes.

Joincake.com— www.joincake.com

This website is the world's largest funeral and end-of-life planning site. It offers:

- online memorials
- a post-loss checklist
- a will-maker
- advanced directive forms
- estate planning documents
- articles on loss and grief

GoFundMe—www.gofundme.com

Registering requires you to:

- provide an email and phone number.
- set your fundraising goal.
- tell your loved one's story.
- add a picture or a video.
- share with friends on social media.
- set a time limit.
- connect your bank account to their platform.

Apply for a funeral loan

This option depends on your family situation. If siblings are involved, applying for a funeral loan may be the most equitable way for the group to cover expenses.

Pros

- A funeral loan is a specific loan designed for funeral expenses. The lender may work directly with the funeral home to ensure the money is used for this purpose.
- Applying for a loan allows you to spread the funeral cost over time in a fixed monthly payment.
- You will get the services you want and the ability to pay when services are rendered.
- You can apply online.

- The lender may offer promotional payment terms like six months at 0% interest.
- Any friend or family member can apply for the loan.
- Several family members can take out a loan together to divide funeral costs and give everyone the option to pay the loan over time. This may be preferable to a single family member placing all charges on their credit card for two reasons: first, the language of the loan may protect the person who signs the contract, and second it may legally bind other family members to be responsible for their share of the cost.

Cons

- As with any loan, there are interest charges.
- It may temporarily give you the feeling that you can spend more than you can afford.
- As with any credit application, you will have a credit check, which may impact your credit score.
- Compare lenders and shop for a reasonable interest rate.
- You are committing to a timeline of a few months to potentially several years. Be sure you have the financial resources to pay off the debt over time.

General recommendations for a funeral loan

- Pay as much as possible upfront at the time of the funeral.
- Don't be tempted to overspend.
- Follow this book's money-saving funeral planning guidelines to reduce the loan amount.
- Be sure to check your interest rate.
- Repay as much as possible during the first few months to shorten your term. www.lendingusa.com

Benefits for families with COVID-19 deaths

FEMA is still providing up to $35,500 *per family* in benefits per application for those who died of COVID-19 at any time since January 20, 2020.

- The maximum for each person is $9,000, and the average amount awarded is $6,500.

- This is a reimbursement plan. You must have paid for the funeral and burial and then file your receipts with FEMA.
- You cannot file online; you must file over the phone.
- If your family has experienced a COVID-19-related death, you are eligible for these benefits, but you should apply soon. This program will end on September 30, 2025.
- The expenses that are eligible for FEMA's plan include the following:
    - burial plot
    - casket
    - urn
    - certifying the death certificate
    - clergy services
    - cremation
    - funeral arrangements
    - headstone
    - interment
    - grave marker

Applicants may apply by calling FEMA at 844-684-6333 from 9 a.m. to 9 p.m. EST, Monday through Friday. Additional information about COVID-19 funeral assistance, including FAQs, is available on FEMA.gov.

Benefits for Veterans: Who is eligible?

If your loved one was in the military, honorably discharged, and possesses a DD214 discharge form, they might be eligible for a cost-free burial in a National Cemetery.

- This will also include a veteran's spouse, a veteran's minor child, and, in some cases, the unmarried adult child of a veteran.
- Veterans may also be eligible for military funeral honors, burial flags, headstones and markers, and Presidential Memorial Certificates at no cost.
- There are *no charges for the plot, vault, or liner, opening or closing the grave, or setting the marker in a national cemetery*; however, the family is responsible for transporting the remains to the cemetery.
- As of 2014, the VA will pay a one-time cash allowance of up to $300 for a non-service-related death and $2000 for a death related to military

service. This is a reimbursement service, so funeral expense receipts must be submitted to claim this benefit.

- Funeral directors have experience with military and veteran burials and can provide additional information and assist you with the process. If it is important to you, inquire about the pricing for this assistance.
- The process is more straightforward if the veteran has pre-planned their burial by securing a pre-need decision letter from the Veterans Administration before death. However, it is possible to secure burial at the time of need; check the VA website for details.

For all the details and forms, call the VA at (855-574-7286) or visit online at—https://www.va.gov/burials-memorials/schedule-a-burial/.

The FTC says: "*You may see ads for so-called 'veterans' specials' by commercial cemeteries. These cemeteries sometimes offer a free plot for the veteran but charge exorbitant rates for an adjoining plot for the spouse and high fees for opening and closing each grave. Evaluate the bottom-line cost to be sure the 'special' is as special as you may be led to believe.*"

If your loved one was the victim of a crime

- All states receive funds via the **Federal Victims of Crime Act (VOCA).**
- These funds from the Office of Victims of Crime (OVC) help support crime victim assistance and compensation programs.
- The National Center for Victims of Crime manages the federal program that compensates crime victims, including funeral costs.
- Benefits vary by state and range from $10,000~$100,000.
- The Center maintains a listing of the programs offered by each state.
- To contact them, call (202-467-8700).

To get information and locate services available in your area, call (855-484-2846) or visit https://ovc.ojp.gov/help-for-victims/terrorism-and-mass-violence

If your loved one was the victim of a disaster

- FEMA assists with funeral expenses if you are in a federally declared disaster area and the death is directly related to the disaster.
- Your state or territory determines the amount you are eligible to receive.

- To qualify, you need to meet the following criteria:
    - You must be a U.S. citizen, non-citizen, or qualified alien.
    - You must have a verifiable identity.
- This is secondary aid. Any burial insurance you possess must be applied first and be insufficient to meet the cost of the disaster-caused death.
- Documentation is required.
- Note that FEMA will only pay costs related to the funeral service and burial. *(See the list in the COVID section above).*
- Items such as flowers and video presentations will not be covered.
- The dollar amount of the award will vary depending on the disaster.
- Call FEMA (800-621-3362) to discuss your circumstances.

Websites to consider if the death is your child

- Children's Burial Assistance—http://childrensburial.org/
- Final Farewell—http://www.finalfarewell.org/
- The TEARS Foundation—https://thetearsfoundation.org/

Additional ways to raise money

- Local non-profits
- Organizations
- Family members
- Local businesses
- Members of your church
- Members of your community

Fundraising options—do what school organizations do

- Organize a bake sale.
- Host a silent auction.
- Sell T-shirts.
- Organize a used book sale.
- Sell boxed mattresses.
- Rent a school cafeteria or church hall and host a dinner sponsored by a local restaurant.
- Organize a community garage sale.

- These activities require some organizing and planning. Enlist friends to help.

Insurance—Burial insurance policies

A word of caution: Not all burial policies are the same, especially policies for seniors purchased late in life. For instance, older seniors may only be eligible for an insurance payout once sufficient premiums have accrued. This is commonly two years after purchasing a burial policy.

A family member recently purchased one of these policies only to learn that she needed to die between years three and six of the policy for it to be beneficial. For every year she lived after year six, she would pay $600 above the $5,000 face value of the policy. If she lived another twenty years, she would pay $13,400 for a $5,000 policy. After we did the numbers, she decided to cancel the policy.

Additionally, when she decided to cancel, she learned that her "thirty-day free look" period began the day she purchased her policy, not the day she received it in the mail. It took the agility of a gymnast to jump through the hoops necessary to cancel the policy within thirty calendar days. Be sure to read all of the fine print.

Another hurdle is the terms set forth in some *General Price Lists*. The fine print on the GPL often states that a *burial policy must have been in force for two years before death* to be considered. In addition, some funeral homes may charge you a 3%-5% fee to process these policies, which may take fourteen to sixty days to pay out. Other funeral homes may require you to secure a short-term loan to cover the face value to ensure their business can be paid immediately. To avoid misunderstandings, if you intend to use one of these policies, be sure to get clarification from the funeral director regarding processing burial insurance before signing a contract.

Life insurance

If you wish to purchase life insurance to pay for your funeral, do an online search to find the best life insurance policy for you. Consider the sites www.policygenius.com or www.selectquote.com. Compare benefits and companies to find the best pricing for your budget. Many burial policies have $5,000-$20,000 or more payouts to help with funeral and burial costs.

Young people should consider taking out a larger whole-life or term life insurance policy to protect their families. For example, a $50,000 term life insurance policy can be purchased for approximately the following monthly premiums according to age:

Male	$10,000	$20,000	$50,000	Female	$50,000
21-25	4.81	8.71	20.43	21-25	11.79
26-30	5.91	10.75	25.28	26-30	15.86
31-35	7.11	12.98	30.62	31-35	20.67
36-40	8.81	16.17	38.28	36-40	25.92
41-45	11.11	20.51	48.73	41-45	32.95
46-50	14.18	26.34	62.83	46-50	43.78
51-55	17.91	33.49	80.21	51-55	55.42
56-60	23.16	43.61	104.9	56-60	70.56
61-65	30.84	58.49	141.44	61-65	90.71
66-70	42.24	80.73	196.23	66-70	119.75
71-75	59.52	114.79	280.54	71-75	165.1
76-80	79.46	154.59	379.98	76-80	236.49

The premiums listed above are samples. Your initial premium is based on your age and health at issue, and premiums will increase as you enter each new five-year age period. Note that premiums for females are slightly lower. Search for a company and policy that is appropriate for your needs and budget. Indeed, $50,000 of insurance and a will can offer significant peace of mind for those willing to consider the unthinkable. If none of the above options apply, your only recourse is to monitor the cost of every item you choose after the death of a loved one.

A note about probate and the estate: If your loved one's estate is large or contains a trust, you must obtain an **EIN** *Employer Identification Number* for estates and trusts. Visit IRS.gov for more information. If the estate is small and several people are either involved in the payment of final expenses or are due to inherit from the estate, a temporary alternative may be to open a new and separate credit card or checking account designated solely for funeral and estate expenses, being mindful that **the deceased social**

security number is no longer valid. This will separate all expenses and make things more straightforward for family members when:

- insurance policies are paid out.
- the deceased's assets are sold.
- reimbursement from other family members is sought.
- taxes must be paid.
- cash inheritances are dispersed.

Summary

After reading this chapter, you may prioritize purchasing an insurance policy. If you have the means to do so and if your parents or single siblings don't have insurance, consider purchasing a policy for each, especially if you will have some financial responsibility for their final expenses. The best and least expensive way to ensure that your funeral will be paid for is by purchasing a $50,000 term insurance policy for you and your family member for less than $20 - $50 per month per month. https://life.selectquote.com/termlife, www.policygenius .com

Just a thought:

We insure everything in our lives: our cars, our homes, our health, and our businesses. We do this to give ourselves peace of mind against an accident, a fire, a weather event, an illness, or a lawsuit. However, most of us are reluctant to insure ourselves, the person whose income allows the ownership of all these things. Life insurance is just that. We are insuring our life against our death to keep our family financially whole in the unfortunate loss of our lives. Why are we so stubborn? The solution is so easy.

Death is scary. But death without life insurance or a will is a nightmare, and the survivors, either you or your family,—never wake up! Maybe it's time?

Notes

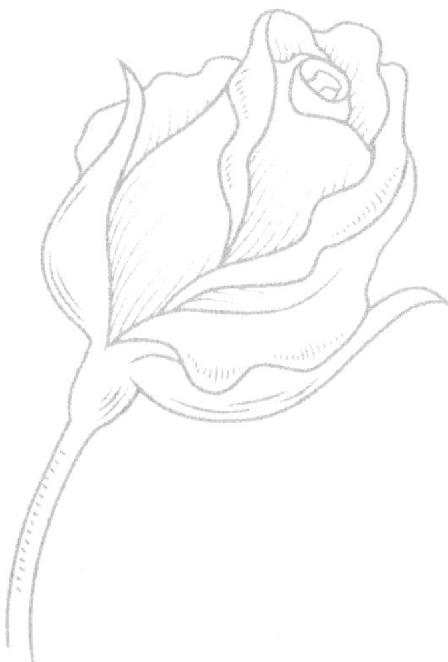

Chapter 16

How Bad Can It Get?
Gloria's Story

- *In 2022, there were 58 million Americans over the age of 65, and this number is expected to increase to 82 million by 2050, which will be 23% of the population.*
- *According to the U.S. Census Bureau, three in ten adults over the age of 65 lived alone in 2022.*
- *Over 17 million seniors over the age of 65 in the U.S. are economically insecure.*

Gloria had been a friend for decades. She had been a teacher in a public school and a freelance musician, and in the years before her death, she taught private piano lessons and music in a preschool. She had been divorced thirty years before her death and had struggled financially for a long time. I was there as she sold her house because she could not afford it, then moved to a condo for a few years where she could give private piano lessons, but then had to let that go when the landlord wanted to sell the property. By then, she struggled to live on her ex-husband's Social Security. She was forced to move to a subsidized apartment for seniors. She insisted on taking her precious baby grand piano with her. After all, music was her life, and her piano was her most prized possession and part of her identity.

This last move sent her into depression, and when a significant car repair bill overwhelmed her, she did not ask for help. She stopped making payments, and her car was repossessed. She would ask for rides, and I could tell her health was failing. I asked if she was seeing a doctor, and she said she was, but even with Medicare, the costs of her prescriptions were high, and I suspect she was skipping doses. She needed a higher level of care but could not afford a private facility.

Gloria had always maintained a large circle of friends, and many gave her regular monetary assistance. One day, I received a call from a mutual friend saying that Gloria had been found dead in her apartment. "Where is her body?" I asked. No one seemed to know. About five of us had remained in touch with her. I called one friend and asked what was going to happen next. She had talked to others, and no one knew what to do or where to start.

One of Gloria's friends had contacted the apartment complex to try to get into her apartment. Management refused because she was not family. They maintained that the apartment complex had to follow strict rules to guard Gloria's privacy and ensure her things were not looted until her family could be notified. Our friend insisted that Gloria had no family in the area and maintained that unless she could get into the apartment and get her address book, no one could contact her family, whom we all knew lived in another city. The facility finally let her in under management's watchful eye. Distant cousins were found about six hundred miles away. They, too, were not in good health and could not afford to come to our city to claim her body or her possessions.

Meanwhile, I was concerned about her final arrangements. Gloria was a deeply religious person, and I felt she needed a church funeral and burial, but first, I had to find her. I contacted the apartment management, who told me she was at the county morgue. I called the morgue, but they could not locate her. After some time, they stated that they had one person named Gloria, but there was a different last name. It seems that even though she was using her maiden name, she had never legally changed her name back after her divorce. I had known her long enough to know her under both names, so I was able to make the connection. Once that mystery was solved, I asked what would happen to her. The coroner responded that if no one claimed her body within thirty days, she would be cremated and buried in a pauper's grave in the county cemetery. That simply could not happen.

The five of us started calling all the people in our networks who knew Gloria, and donations began to pour in. I went to a local funeral home to ask for assistance, which they were kind enough to grant. They offered a reduced price for the cremation, picked up our dear friend from the county morgue, transported her to the crematorium, and returned her ashes to me. Meanwhile, they filed the paperwork for the death certificate. *This was a wonderful example of compassion from a funeral home in her hour of need.*

I next went to the cemetery to ask for assistance and was told what I had to do to keep the costs to a minimum. I then spoke to the pastor of my church, who not only donated his services, the church, and the printing of Gloria's funeral program but agreed to pay the cemetery costs as well. Members of the choir gave the gift of song. I planned the service, created a program, and wrote a eulogy. Another friend found a picture, enlarged it for the service, kept everyone apprised of the plans, and collected donations. Another bought flowers. Gloria's cousins could not attend the funeral, but many of Gloria's friends were present. After the funeral, I sent her death certificate and mementos of the funeral to her family. Unfortunately, this happened before COVID-19, so the concept of the virtual funeral had not yet been initiated in our church.

As a friend and a musician, I wanted to retrieve Gloria's piano so it could be donated, but the rules regarding possessions at the apartment complex were strict. The management told me that if no family member came to claim her possessions within thirty days, they would be destroyed. Since the piano was heavy, it would be dropped over the balcony of the second floor, and the pieces would be placed in the dumpster along with all of her other possessions. One of Gloria's friends reported that the piano had been damaged in the move to the apartment and suspected that the soundboard had been cracked. I could not witness the destruction of that instrument, so I left the subject alone.

Summary

We can only imagine how often this happens to elderly persons in the U.S. who have no money, have lost touch with or outlived their families, or whose families cannot afford an unexpected expense of any amount. These bodies go unclaimed and are left at the county morgue, as I discovered when trying to retrieve Gloria's remains. Fortunately, Gloria had lots of friends.

Here are some statistics on seniors and poverty

- There were 55,892,014 seniors over the age of sixty-five in the U.S. in 2022, which was 16.8% of the population.
- Over 10.3% of these seniors are living below the poverty line, earning less than $25,760 per year.
- In the U.S., 40%—or 22,357,000 seniors live on Social Security alone.
- According to the U.S. Census Bureau, 1,000,000 more seniors aged sixty-five years and older fell into poverty in 2021.
- Seniors were the ONLY GROUP that suffered a rise in poverty, and it is the highest it has been in twenty years.

These statistics are troubling for a country that is among the wealthiest in the world. If you know someone who is elderly and alone, connect with them and try to find out if there is anyone whom they would like to be contacted if they become seriously ill.

If you are alone—who would help? Can someone find your addresses and important phone numbers?

In our digital world, most people no longer have address books. I recently left my phone at a retail establishment on the night before a 6:30 a.m. flight. In the rush of last-minute packing and chores, it was 9:30 p.m. before I realized my phone was missing. It was eye-opening to realize that the only phone numbers I had written down were those of my children, who could not help me at that moment. I had purchased a non-refundable flight with rewards, and I needed to speak to an agent so I could re-book my flight with the least financial impact. I knocked on a neighbor's door at 10 p.m. and asked her to use her phone so I could call the airline to change my flight. The next morning, I had to wait until the store opened to retrieve my phone, which was several hours after my flight had departed.

My point is, how would you help someone—or even yourself—when family contacts are stored in the digital vault known as your phone? Maybe it is time to revive the old-fashioned address book and write out the phone numbers that would be most helpful in an emergency or after a death. If Gloria had not had an address book, her family would never have known what happened to her. Also, it's time to be sure someone has the passcode to your phone and other digital accounts. One more thing to add to your "to-do" list.

Phone numbers, addresses, and passwords are critical to those who will close out your life. One night, while you're watching TV, take the time to write important phone numbers in an old-fashioned address book or in a spreadsheet and store them with your important papers.

Notes

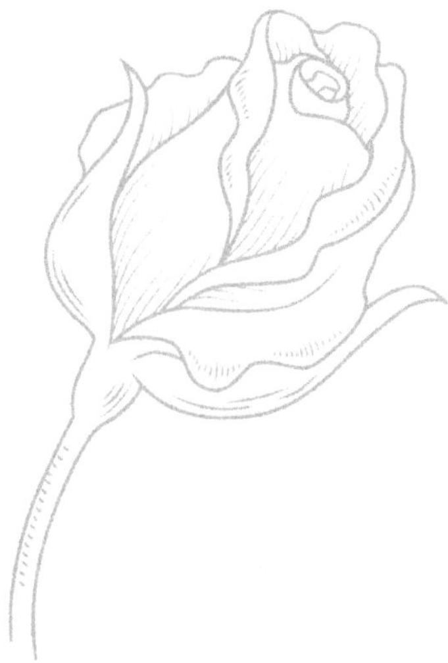

Chapter 17

Documents to Gather – The Physical, Financial, and Digital World of the Deceased

- *Documents to find to close out your loved one's life.*
- *Companies and financial entities that need to be contacted in the coming weeks.*
- *Accounts that need to be transferred or closed to prevent identity theft.*

By now, you are emotionally wrung out and physically exhausted, but unfortunately, there is much more to do. It is important to say that you need to take time to grieve, and although there are deadlines in settling the estate, use these suggestions to make your own list and then methodically tackle one issue at a time. Confronting these tasks in small groups may help you feel less overwhelmed with the process. After all, it's time to go back to the people and responsibilities of your life.

Documents to gather

The primary documents you need to find include the following:

- Password book or digital password vault
- A will
- Social Security card or number
- Insurance policies
- Tax documents
- Past tax returns
- Bank account information including, checking, savings, IRAs, and CDs
- Checking and savings account statements for the last twelve months. This will give you an overview of earnings vs. spending
- Credit union accounts. Statements may show direct deposit income and bill payment patterns
- Credit cards and statements of each card for twelve months
- Student loan lender and statements
- Investment accounts
- Safe deposit box information and keys
- Pension accounts
- Marriage license
- Mortgage company and statements
- Homeowners insurance
- Auto loan company
- Auto insurer
- Pay stub if the deceased was still employed
- Passport
- Driver's license
- Deeds and titles to your property and vehicles

Who should be notified when a single person passes away?

Employer

- Claim any unpaid wages.
- Notify colleagues.
- Determine if there are any benefits that might be paid.
- Inquire if there is a life insurance policy from the employer.
- Secure personal possessions.

Mortgage company

- Make payment arrangements.
- Contact the homeowner's insurance company to determine renewals.
- Determine what taxes are paid and when they are due.
- Secure the property.
- Decide how to handle the utilities and notify those companies.
- Notify the landlord, if the deceased was renting.

Credit card companies

- Credit card companies should be notified, and the cards should be closed immediately.
- Determine the amount of debt owed. Existing debt will be paid from the assets of the estate.
- Identify and cancel recurring charges and subscriptions.
- Notify credit reporting agencies to monitor possible fraud.
    - Equifax.com (888-766-0008)
    - Experian.com (888-397-3742)
    - TransUnion.com (800-680-7289)

Insurance companies

- Health insurance to terminate payments
- Cancel vision/dental insurance
- Life insurance company to collect benefits
- Homeowners insurance
- Car insurance
- Renters insurance

Financial institutions

- Banks: checking and savings accounts
    - Identify monthly ACH or auto-payments to utilities, mortgage, insurance payments, loans, and credit card payments. Discuss with the bank how these drafts should be handled.
    - Research and cancel direct payments and subscriptions that are no longer needed, such as Amazon Prime, Netflix, Hulu, etc.
    - Investigate beneficiary designations on each account.
    - Look for IRA accounts and CDs.
    - Determine if there is a safe deposit box.
- Credit unions
- Investment accounts
- Retirement accounts

Lenders

- Notify institutions to set terms to settle outstanding financial debts.
- Personal loans
- Car loan lender
- Home equity lender
- Student loans - see information below

Utilities and monthly home-related accounts to close or transfer

- Gas/water/ sewer companies
- Electric company
- Cell phone or landline carrier to close accounts
- Cable TV provider
- Internet provider
- Garbage or recycling
- Newspapers/magazines

Pension entities

- Contact the Social Security Administration if benefits change for a spouse or if you have minor children (1-800-772-1213).
- Contact Veterans Affairs if applicable.

- Contact federal or state pension funds if the deceased worked for a state or federal government. Check if there is an insurance policy or death benefit hidden here.

Miscellaneous

- Contact the pharmacy to cancel auto-refills of prescriptions.
- Notify the election board to remove the name from the voter registration roll— cancel memberships, gym, etc.
- Condo or HOA associations to determine their fees and due dates.
- Contact the U.S. Post Office to cancel or forward mail. However, ensure you receive all tax documents sent in January online or by mail. You will need to file the final tax return to close the estate.
- Contact the Department of Motor Vehicles to cancel the driver's license to prevent identity theft.
- Secure all intellectual property, including copyrighted material, domain names, trademarks, copyrights, websites, blogs, YouTube accounts, or computer code that the deceased may have written, owned, or managed.
- Close online businesses, eBay, Etsy, Amazon, YouTube, etc.

Secure hardware, computers, external hard drives, flash drives, tablets, smartphones, e-readers, digital cameras, and other digital devices. www.everplans.com

Digital accounts

- Close all online banking and investment accounts.
- Close email accounts.
- Close social media accounts.
- Unsubscribe from newsletters.
- Secure video gaming accounts.
- Secure online cloud storage accounts, especially photos.
- Close or transfer online accounts —Amazon, Netflix, etc.
- Cancel all digital subscriptions and recurring charges.

Student loans

- **Federal student loans qualify for student loan discharge when the borrower dies.** The remaining balance will be forgiven, so no one in your family will become responsible for your debt after you are gone.
- Parent PLUS loans are also discharged upon the death of the student or the death of the parent.
- Federal Grad PLUS and Federal Parent PLUS loans are discharged even if they have an endorser.
- **Private student loans MAY or MAY NOT be forgiven.** Loan forgiveness is not required of private lenders.
- A co-signer may become responsible for the loan balance on a private loan. Contact your lender. https://www.bankrate.com

If your loved one had minimal or no assets

- Check credit card statements and notify creditors.
- Determine if there is a car loan and notify the lender.
- Determine if there is other debt.

Secure all tangible property

- Jewelry, sterling flatware, fine china, artwork, furniture, tools, and equipment all have value in an estate. Do not allow family members to begin to take items without knowing the value of those items. Call an appraiser if necessary.
- All items should be inventoried, and the value assessed. Some family members may prefer to get tools and equipment, and others may not wear jewelry or have room for furniture but may need cash. The inheritance must be equitable, whether it is real property or money.
- To avoid problems, hold off on property distributions to heirs until the estate has been closed.

WARNING:

Why should I continue to make mortgage and car payments? I can't afford to do this!

Note: Not making a car payment may result in repossession of the car, and not making mortgage payments can result in the foreclosure of your home. Why does this matter? Unless the house or car was recently purchased, each might have significant equity in them. If the house was purchased for $150,000 a few years ago, there may have been a sizeable down payment, and the payments may have reduced the principal, but more importantly, the house may have increased in value. Once the estate is settled, this is valuable cash.

> *If you stop making mortgage payments, don't pay the taxes, or let the insurance lapse, the house may go into foreclosure. When that happens, the lender will sell the property, and all equity will go to the lender.*

Granted, you did not have to make more monthly payments, but you can no longer sell the home to retrieve the equity, which may be a substantial part of the estate. Be sure to call the mortgage company, an estate attorney, or an accountant to learn the consequences of foreclosure. The same is true of the car. The deceased may have made a sizeable down payment or even paid a large cash deposit for the vehicle. Allowing it to be repossessed for a few remaining payments may be surrendering a significant amount of cash.

While settling the estate, keep good records

Settling an estate is a complicated, long-term process, and it won't be possible to remember all the details of each call months from the death. Keeping records takes additional time, but having a system will save time and frustration in the coming months. Consider purchasing a dedicated covered file box with a lid and a handle for storing documents in folders and a notebook with a page or two dedicated to each account you find to record calls, contacts and questions. Be sure to:

- Keep a diary of all the calls you make.
- List the account, account number, and company phone number.
- Write down the questions you want to ask.
- Record the name of the person you speak to.
- Take notes on each call that you make.

- Take the time to develop a filing system as you gather documents.

- Make a copy of all statements and documents that need attention. Keep the originals separate from the working documents so you have a backup if anything is lost or misplaced.

- Keep all the copies of financial statements or documents in one place, in file folders. This will save valuable time searching for papers when questions arise.

- As the tax documents come in, place them in a tax folder.

- Use the lists above as your guide, and then make your own.

This list is a generic outline of what to look for after the funeral. It is not complete but is intended to trigger what to look for and should give you a starting point as you organize the documents and accounts that are pertinent to probate.

Summary

As you can see, there is still much to be done. Locate as many documents as you can immediately after the death. Understand that unless the deceased has a spouse, it is likely that their estate will have to go through probate. Rest assured that *unless you are an estate attorney, no one knows how to do this.*

To start the probate process, call the county clerk where the person lived on the day of death. You will need to file the will, if there is one, and present the death certificate. At that point, an executor will be appointed. If there is no will, an administrator will be appointed. It is best to do this as soon as you receive the death certificate. Procrastination may result in the loss or misplacement of critical documents or, depending on the laws of your state, may result in fines for missing deadlines later on.

It is important to gather and organize all financial paperwork, deeds, and tax documents. These are common to all estates, large or small, and the process of gathering documents is the same whether or not there is a will. Creating a recording and filing system is the secret to saving time, minimizing frustration, and getting the job done efficiently.

Understand that procrastination is your enemy. Gather as much information as you can as quickly as you can to dissipate your discomfort with the probate process.

This section is intended for informational purposes only. It does not constitute legal or financial advice or opinion. For specific questions, contact an accountant or an estate attorney.

Notes

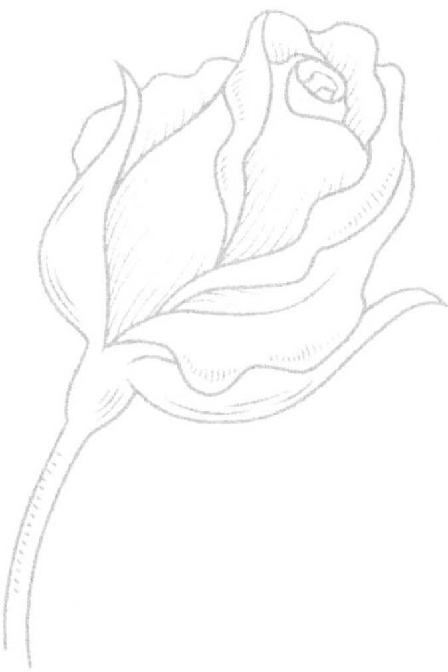

Chapter 18

What Have We Learned?

Funeral myths that we all accept without question

- **Myth 1:** *You think your deceased loved one deserves the best money can buy for their funeral.*
- **Myth 2:** *Cremations are always cheaper than funerals with burials.*
- **Myth 3:** *You accept "the code of silence of the bereaved:" Do not ever discuss the cost of a funeral after the fact because it will be seen as a sign of disrespect for your loved one.*

Myth 1: You think your loved one deserves the best money can buy, and you want to show your family and friends how much you cared for them.

Debunked: Caring for your loved one is over. Caring for your family is now your priority. The public part of the funeral and burial lasts a maximum of two days. Will your friends and family pay for these deluxe goods as you financially struggle over the next year or two? Of course not. You will be on your own. Keep in mind, it's only two days of shame—you can weather it.

Myth 2: Cremations are always cheaper than funerals with burials.

Debunked: Do NOT buy into the myth that cremations are always cheaper than burials.

- Funeral homes know that you accept this myth and have devised creative and sometimes deceptive pricing packages that keep cremation costs high and often reduce services. They have to disclose this in the *General Price List*, but if you never look at one, you'll never know what was missing or added, and you'll pay whatever the invoice says.
- If you are considering cremation, do a cost analysis of all cremation pricing on the GPL, including the packages. Be sure to identify what is and is not included under each category.
- If there is only one choice for cremation, it may indicate straightforward pricing.
- Use the **Funeral Home Price Comparison Worksheet** in *Appendix* B for your analysis of cremation pricing.
- Buyer beware! Do your research. Reread *Chapter* 14.

Myth 3: The code of silence of the bereaved: Do not ever discuss the cost of a funeral after the fact because it will be seen as a sign of disrespect for your loved one.

Debunked: Says who? Your great-grandmother? The funeral director?

Discussing funeral pricing:

- is not your shame to bear. It shines a light on the unreasonable cost of death.
- is an indictment of funeral industry pricing and practices, not you and your family.

- breaks the silence that allows the funeral industry to continue to put profit over people and grow wealthier at your expense.
- illuminates the financially destabilizing effect funeral costs have on families.
- may encourage your family and friends to make a plan.

Speak up and warn your children, family, and friends and encourage them to get prepared. Buy them a copy of this book and have a family discussion before it's too late.

Here is what we have learned:

About death

- Death can steal your time, money, home, possessions, business, financial security, and your children's well-being.
- Death is often unexpected, affecting all demographics—young and old, rich and poor.
- The moment you take your last breath ends your ability to protect your family unless you have made a plan and made it legal.
- An unplanned death can become a real burden for you or your loved ones.
- Death can be the beginning of a period of financial chaos for the family you have left behind, quickly revealing the thoughtlessness of your procrastination.
- **Refusing to think about death does not keep it from striking**. It just makes your family more vulnerable to its lethal blows.

About funerals

- Funerals and burials can be so expensive that they can financially devastate your family.
- Every time the funeral director asks you a question, and nod in acceptance, costs can accumulate. Think of the rolling tally of the gas pump.
- The moment a funeral director picks up your loved one, there is a presumption that they will handle all funeral arrangements. Do your research before you make that call. Changing your mind may lead to added fees.

- Funeral directors will guide you toward a full-service traditional funeral unless you have a plan and are assertive in keeping it.

About how to control funeral costs

- Shop for a funeral home before you need one.
- Insist on obtaining a copy of the *General Price List*—it may lead to more transparent pricing— because even if you succumb to less-than-transparent tactics, you will be able to prove it later.
- Take a hard look at cremation vs. burial if cost is a factor for you.
- Determine what goods and services you want before meeting with a funeral director and dismiss the rest.
- Become an informed consumer to resist being upsold expensive goods or services.

About your rights with funeral homes

The only way to reduce funeral costs at the time of a death is to know your rights and understand funeral pricing. You have the right to:

- walk into any funeral home in the country and ask for a *General Price List*, a *Casket Price List*, and a *Burial Container Price List*. Understand that prices may change every six to twelve months.
- visit a funeral home, obtain price lists, and return to your car in five to seven minutes without giving your name or sitting for a consultation.
- examine all itemized prices before you sign a contract. You cannot do this without a *General Price List* to ensure there are no less expensive options.
- research a casket or an urn online and ask the funeral director for a price match. If he does not agree to do it, you can purchase the item online and have it delivered to the funeral home without fees or consequences.
- compare all package prices with the itemized costs of the individual items included in each.

About funeral directors

Your state authorizes funeral directors to maintain the chain of custody of a deceased body from death until interment. This function is for the health and well-being of society. Funeral directors:

- transport the deceased from the place of death and store the body until burial or cremation.
- gather the information for the death certificate, file it with the county, and obtain the necessary permits for cremation or interment.
- must be paid before services are rendered.
- have an unfair advantage by having custody of your loved one when you are vulnerable and mentally compromised in making decisions.
- count on you not thinking about death until you meet them. This makes you more vulnerable and more likely to purchase whatever they offer.
- can be businesspeople dealing in compassion or compassionate people who serve the grieving. The only way to find the latter is to visit their business before you need them.
- gain your trust when you are most vulnerable making you comfortable spending more money than you can afford.

> ***Funeral directors can be—businesspeople dealing in compassion or compassionate people who serve the grieving.***

About questions you should ask a funeral director before you sign a contract

- *(If you purchased a package for burial or cremation)*– Are there any items I will have to purchase besides those listed in this package?
- Is the crematory fee included?
- Is a cremation container included? How much am I paying for that?
- What is the least expensive cremation container you sell?
- Do you charge a fee to return ashes to the funeral home?
- Is an outer burial container included in the burial package price?
- Are there any unexpected cemetery fees?
- Am I paying for a reception that I may not want?
- Is there a fee to use my credit card?

- Do you charge to process insurance policies? Here is my policy. What can I expect in terms of delays and fees?
- Can I see an invoice for what I would like to purchase *before* I sign the contract?
- Will you sign my invoice to ensure that there will be no additional charges on the final invoice?

About funeral costs

- You are likely to be financially blindsided if the first time you think about the cost of a funeral is one hour after a death.
- Funerals are expensive, costing $8,000–$20,000 or more.
- **Do not ever plan a funeral without a *General Price List* in your hand!**
- Once the funeral director picks up your loved one, you will incur the *Basic Services Fee* from that funeral home. The price for this service ranges from $1,800–$5,000 in different areas of the country. The cost of the funeral escalates from this baseline fee.
- The only person liable for the cost of a funeral is the one who signs the contract.
- To reduce the cost of a funeral at the time of death, you need help from a trusted friend or relative as an *Advocate* to act as your business manager. Encourage this person to gather and compare funeral home and cemetery pricing on the day following a death.
- Discussing the cost of a funeral with friends and family is not disrespectful to your loved one; rather, it may expose some questionable practices of the funeral industry and warns the people you care about.

  A funeral and burial can cost as much as a new car. Yet over 85% of the population finances a new car purchase. However, this privilege is not extended to a family who has suffered a death and incurred an expense in the tens of thousands of dollars, often without warning. How did this happen?

About cemeteries

- Burials are expensive. They are not included in the price of a funeral and may cost from a few hundred dollars to $40,000.
- To be buried in a cemetery, you must:
  - purchase a plot.
  - purchase a grave liner or vault in addition to a casket.

- pay opening and closing grave *interment fees.*
- purchase a marker or monument.

- The FTC's *Funeral Rule* does NOT cover cemeteries, and if you are not careful, pricing for a burial can quickly get out of control due to numerous *not-so-transparent* fees.
- Like funerals, all costs and fees associated with a burial must be paid before services are rendered.

About cremation

- Cremation or donating a body to science are ways to reduce funeral and burial costs.
- Direct Cremation or Immediate Burial may be your least expensive options.
- Cremation by a dedicated cremation facility may be the best way to reduce costs.
- Choosing a direct cremation facility and using the CHECKLIST provided in *Chapter* 5 enables you to plan your funeral without a funeral director by using your church, fraternal hall, community center, or park to celebrate your funeral.
- The number of cremations is rising every year as families attempt to control the cost of death.
- Be aware that cremation can be more expensive than a burial if you do not read all of the fine print listed on the *General Price List.*
- Cremation packages may cost as much as a full-service funeral.
- You may be paying for items that you do not want or use in a cremation package. Read the fine print.
- Do not purchase a cremation package without comparing all items needed with the itemized price on the GPL.
- Ask the funeral director if additional items that are not included in the package you are considering will be required.
- Cremations are expected to exceed 70% of all deaths by 2030.

About money and death

- Funerals and burials must be paid in full before services are rendered.
- Over 80% of Americans do not have enough savings to pay for a funeral and burial within seven to ten days of a death when the payment is due.

- Over 55% of Americans go into debt when they experience a family death.
- Over 62% of people who experience a death maintain that they cannot grieve appropriately due to the effects that the cost of a funeral has on their mental health.
- You cannot use a deceased person's credit cards or checking accounts after they pass. If you do so, you risk charges of fraud.
- When you place funeral costs on a credit card, you have to consider four things:
    - the rate of interest on the card.
    - the current amount of debt you are carrying overall.
    - the length of time it will take to pay off this additional debt.
    - whether the funeral home charges you an upfront service fee for using a credit card.

About Social Security and death

- Social Security can be triggered upon death even if you are not at retirement age.
- It is available to the following family members after a death:
    - Surviving children under sixteen or eighteen if still in high school.
    - Surviving spouses over sixty.
    - Surviving spouses aged fifty with a disability.
    - Children over eighteen if they became disabled before age twenty-two.
    - Ex-spouses who were married for ten years and are eligible for retirement.
    - Deceased worker's parents, age sixty-two or older, if the worker supported them.

About what should NOT be included in your will or placed in your safe deposit box

You may need these documents at the end of your life before you pass away and definitely before your will is read. (*All of these will be discussed in detail in Book II*).

- **Plans for your end-of-life medical needs**
  - Health care directives—documents you need while you are ALIVE but nearing death.
  - Long-term care insurance policies that might be needed for end-of-life care.
  - Health insurance cards, Medicare card, Social Security card, and other important documents that might be needed for your care.
  - A medical power of attorney - a person designated to make medical decisions for you if you cannot make them yourself.
  - Durable power of attorney - a person designated to pay your bills and make financial decisions for you if you are incapacitated.
- **Plans for your funeral**
  - Your desire to be buried or cremated.
  - Your wishes for your funeral service.
  - Outline for your obituary, including your lineage from your grandparents to great-grandchildren.
  - Cemetery information.
  - Life information, including a timeline of your employment and important life events.
  - People to be called or included in your funeral service.
- **Plans to pay for your funeral**
  - A contract for a pre-paid funeral or cremation plan.
  - The existence and location of a burial or life insurance policy.
  - Bank accounts designated to pay for your final expenses.
  - Accounts with payable-on-death beneficiaries assigned to people you trust.
  - Life insurance policies allocated for end-of-life expenses.

Summary

- If you want your wishes honored after your death—write them out.
- If you don't want your family to have to pay for your final expenses— pay for them yourself. Either pre-pay for these services, set money aside in a joint account with beneficiary designations, or buy an insurance policy.
- If you know how you want your worldly possessions dispersed —write a will.
- If you don't have a lot of money but want your family to maintain their standard of living after you die—buy a life insurance policy.

Remember, a death without a plan becomes a burden to your family.

Chapter 19

Assessing Your Readiness for a Death in Your Family

- *Death is a multi-faceted loss, and the data reports that 3.4 million people died in the U.S. in 2023.*
- *This is an average of 9,500 individuals per day.*
- *Conservative statistics state that for every death in the U.S., a minimum of five people are left grieving.*

We are all aware that this heartache does not last just a week, but it can go on for many, many months. Grief is insidious and complicated. It erupts in the most unexpected ways. Now factor in that this number increases by 45,000 heartbroken individuals every day! The deaths will not stop, and the sorrow will not stop, and unfortunately, the consequences of the costs of that death could linger for years. It seems reasonable to expect that families have the right to celebrate their loved ones and mourn their loss without losing their entire nest egg or taking on thousands of dollars of debt.

There are only two ways to confront death—and it's completely your choice.

- Passively
  - Don't think about death until it happens because it will be years from now, and you have plenty of time.
  - But if it does happen, let the funeral director guide you through the process, handle every detail for you, and then pay the bill.
  - Likewise, don't take the time to write a will. Your state has all the tools it needs to distribute your money and property and to assign care for your children.

- Proactively
  - Take charge and develop your own plan for a family death—and hope you never need it.
  - This plan will help you control the cost of your funeral and even freeze it if paid decades before your death.
  - It gives you the freedom to arrange care for your children and expediently distribute your money and property as you wish.

The only control we have over death is to prepare for it before it occurs. Otherwise, we are just victims. Victims of our sorrow and emotions, victims of the destabilization of our lives, victims of the laws of our state, and, in some cases, victims of an industry that capitalizes on our loss.

This book has been dedicated to helping you become proactive. It informed you of the logistics of navigating a funeral, including what to expect after death, tasks to complete, and how to plan a celebration of life.

You now know that controlling funeral costs can be done in various ways, from challenging the paradigms of the traditional funeral to restructuring your idea of a *perfect* one and then shopping for a funeral home that will best suit your needs. As a family, you have the right to celebrate your loved one and mourn their passing, but it is also your right not to be financially devastated after your loss, and you can only do this by being proactive. It's time to assess what you need to do to immunize your family against the worst-case scenario.

Assess the cost of your final expenses

As an individual, you cannot change the prices charged by funeral homes, but by now, you know that you have options to control these costs.

Solution: For example, you can:

- decide which funeral services you want before a death occurs, starting with cremation vs. burial.
- refuse to purchase funeral goods without seeing a *General Price List* so you can compare itemized prices of goods to package prices.
- pre-plan and pre-pay for these services and purchase a cemetery plot before you need it.

Assess how much a funeral costs in your area

You can't compare prices if you don't possess copies of GPLs from competing businesses. According to the *Funeral Rule*, you now know that you must be given a *General Price List* if you walk into a funeral home and specifically ask for one. Still, my observation and personal experience is that in many cases, *you will not* be given a GPL if you try to get it by mail or email.

Solution: Shop for funeral prices in your neighborhood by securing *General Price Lists* and selecting a funeral home before you need one. Then, use the **Funeral Home Price Comparison Worksheet** found in *Appendix* B to document and compare the prices from the GPLs you have secured. Using the information you obtained, determine how to design a funeral within your financial parameters.

Obtaining funeral price lists. Your script—it's really this simple!

1. Drive to the funeral home.
2. Park your car.
3. Walk inside.
4. Then say the following:

"Could I please get a copy of your price list?" "Does this price list include the price of caskets and burial containers? (*If the answer is no*). "Could I please get a copy of those prices, too? Is this a family-owned funeral home?"

5. Thank them, walk out, and go back to your car.
6. Repeat the exercise.

This exchange takes less than two minutes, and I promise you it is this simple, but it is critical. It may be a new and uncomfortable exercise for you, but I guarantee that every funeral home in the U.S. knows the federal law and will oblige you. After all, how do they know you are not a secret shopper doing routine inspections for the FTC? Remember, it is likely that *you will not* be given a *General Price List* if you try to get one by mail or email, and you may not get the complete picture if you try to obtain prices over the phone. https://www.ftc.gov/news-events/news/press-releases/2022/10/ftc-seeks-improve-american-publics-access-funeral-service-prices-online

Assess how your family would handle the days following your death

- Have you been clear about your preference for burial or cremation?
- Do they know what you would like your end-of-life service to be like?
- Have you told them that they can shop for price lists from multiple funeral homes?
- If you have already shopped, have you informed them which funeral home you would use?
- Have you left instructions regarding how your final arrangements will be paid?
- Have you purchased a cemetery plot if you want a physical burial?
- Have you shared your choices with close family members?

Solution: Make time to gather funeral information in your area. Finalize your decisions and create important end-of-life documents. Write down your personal plan and preferences for your funeral, including how to pay for it. Discuss your choices with your spouse or other family members, or at the very least, write them down and put them where they will be found near or after your death. If you are close to death, you still have time to create important documents if you or your loved one needs to. Don't squander this valuable gift of time.

Assess your financial situation:

- Are you in debt?
- Do you have any savings?
- Are you living paycheck to paycheck?
- How would your family survive if your income or your spouse's income disappeared?
- Do you know how much a funeral costs in your area?
- Do you know how your final expenses would be paid?
- How would your family stay financially afloat until the probate process is complete and all your creditors are paid?

Solution: Buy life insurance. This way, you can use someone else's money to solve this problem. Think of it this way: Would you think twice if you could spend fifty dollars a month to get $50,000 on the worst day of your family's life? How about the equivalent of your car payment to get $250,000, $500,000, or even a million dollars in the weeks following your death? Purchasing life insurance is not a lump sum cost but a monthly budget item. You probably pay several hundred dollars every month to have the convenience of using a car. If eating at home one more time each week would give your family this kind of security, would you do it? Money does not relieve you of your anguish, but it does help you or your family move forward with life.

Assess how well you are protected legally

- Do you have a will?
- Have you set up guardianships for your children?
- Have you set up a medical or durable power of attorney?

Solution: Create all of the documents listed above so that a plan is in place when that awful day arrives. Your spouse, parents, siblings, or your children will be so grateful that they are not forced to make these difficult decisions for you. Or worse yet, they do not have to clean up the loose ends/mess of your life by spending months in a probate court, figuring out how to finance your home so that it can be sold rather than repossessed, and deciding who will raise your children.

Assess your medical vulnerability

Consider if you were a victim of a car accident or a mass shooting and were incapacitated and needed medical care. You are still alive, but you can't take care of yourself.

- Do you want to bankrupt your family by being kept on life support for months?
- You need someone to make medical decisions for you—your heart has stopped multiple times in the last week. Do you want to keep being revived? Or both of your lungs were punctured, and you need a double lung transplant. Can your insurance pay for that? Who has the legal authority to decide this?
- You may not have a spouse or significant other to pay your mortgage, insurance, and other monthly expenses, but these bills need to be paid. Money is still coming in, but no one has the authority to access it.

Solution: Create important end-of-life documents.

- A **healthcare directive**
- A **medical power of attorney**
- A **durable power of attorney**

> ***If you plan ahead, someone you trust can take care of everything, and if you recover, the power assigned to this individual reverts back to you.***

Assess how your family would handle the weeks following your death

- Can all of your essential legal documents be found, i.e., your will, business documents, estate plan, deeds, and titles?

- Can your passwords be found?
- If you have a safe, does someone have the code?
- If you have a safe deposit box, does someone have signatory privileges and access to the key?

Solution: Organize your financial statements and legal documents in one place. Make sure you have a safe place for them, especially if you are at a high risk for natural disasters. Incalculable information can be lost, and immeasurable hours can be spent by your family trying to reconstruct this jigsaw puzzle. How would you feel if the task was assigned to *you*?

A thought about end-of-life documents

I have not discussed wills, estate plans, powers of attorney, and healthcare directives in depth in this book, but if you are faced with trying to settle an estate without them, you will be a victim of death's second blow—the probate court. Trying to settle an estate under these circumstances can consume your time and rob you of your assets or those of the deceased.

This subject will be discussed at length in a sequel to this book, but my advice to you is to get a will written before you wait to read about it. Note that a will should be considered right up there with other important documents in your life, like your birth certificate, your passport, driver's license, and your Social Security card, but it is the only document you don't need until after you take your last breath, so there's no urgency, right?

> ***The problem is that dying without a will is a devastating, expensive, and complicated waste of time for your surviving family members.***

However, don't take my word for it. One or more of your friends has walked through this. Take the time to listen to their story if you need to be convinced.

> ***The converse is also true: having a will is the most thoughtful, loving, and considerate gift you can give your family in the weeks following your death.***

It allows them to "just grieve." Decisions have been made, your wishes are clear, money is available, your home has been transferred, potential family conflicts are dissolved, and court appearances and legal fees are minimized.

My end-of-life plan—a minimalist approach

After spending almost two years writing this book, I feel the urgency to get my own life in order, and I have decided to share my end-of-life plan. I have searched for the least expensive way to do this. Since I, like you, do not know when or where my life will end, I want to create the most flexible plan for my children, so I have made the following decisions.

Final arrangements:

- After resisting cremation, I finally convinced myself that I would be dead when they light that fire, so I won't feel a thing. This gives me a lot of flexibility as I age. I travel a great deal, and this way, I don't have to worry about dying in the wrong state or country. It also gives my children the flexibility to mail my ashes to my hometown for burial.
- I have purchased a *Direct Cremation* from a funeral home and am making monthly payments, so it is a monthly budget item for me.
- A funeral and visitation are important to me unless I live until my 90s, when few friends or relatives will be alive to attend. The outline of my funeral service, including Scripture selections and music, is with other important papers.
- With my cremains in hand, my children can plan my visitation, funeral, and reception through either my city church or my country church.
- I plan to be buried in a family plot in my hometown cemetery, so I will only have to pay $200 to open and close the grave. I spoke to the caretaker of the cemetery, and he reassured me that no other fees were involved. I should also note that the cost of a single plot was only $500 in my small hometown. This was insignificant compared to the $1,300 to bury an urn in the local urban cemetery, which did not include the $3,500 cost of the plot. But what if you didn't know things like this after your spouse's or parent's sudden death? My guess is that you would pay the bill and deal with the financial fallout over the next few months—or longer.

Final expenses: The total cost of my funeral will be:

- Cremation–$1,950 (Direct Cremation - including transportation of my remains, death certificate, cremation and crematory fee, cremation container, and one for my ashes).
- Funeral—$750- $1,000 for the use of a church for a visitation, funeral, stipends for clergy and musicians, and a reception.
- The cost to mail my ashes to my hometown using the U.S. Postal Service will be $30.
- Urn–$100.
- Opening and closing the grave in my small-town church cemetery –$200.
- Cremation vault for an urn–$100.
- Flat grave marker–$250–$800.
- The total cost should be less than $3,500 for my cremation, funeral, and burial of my cremains, plus the cost of a marker.

Financial paperwork: Each year, when I gather documents for my taxes, I place all of my end-of-year statements in a single file folder. It's a shortcut to have all of my accounts and financial information in one place, including account numbers, balances, and phone numbers. However, now that I want a more permanent solution, I will create a spreadsheet with all of this information on one sheet of paper and place it with my will.

A will: Before I went overseas in March 2020, there was some talk of a virus that might get out of control, so I hastily updated my will through an online will maker. It gave me great peace of mind during my three months in quarantine in a foreign country during COVID-19. However, I now have a sense of urgency to have a will written by an estate attorney and will finish this before I publish this book and go abroad again.

Estate plan: While visiting the estate attorney for my new will, I also decided I needed an estate plan to make transferring my assets and selling my home easy for my children. This plan will also include my healthcare directives and medical and durable powers of attorney.

Insurance policies:

- I worked for a state government, and I have a life insurance policy that will pay out upon my death.

- I set up a pre-payment plan for my cremation.
- I have a MASA air ambulance insurance policy that will return my body to the U.S. without cost if I die while traveling.
- Similar plans are also available through travel insurance, some direct cremation facilities, and funeral homes. However, by purchasing this policy independently, I also have coverage for emergency medical transport overseas and within the U.S. https://getmasa.com/.
- I also purchased a long-term care policy in case I need to be admitted to an assisted living facility or need in-home care as I age.

Beneficiary designations: Checked, and bingo, I found one account with no beneficiaries listed—be sure to check each account.

Passwords: Documented and in a safe place with other important papers.

It's time to finish this! I still have some things to do, but I am close. I should also note that periodically, as your life changes, you may need to revisit and revise these plans.

Summary

Sobering thoughts—have you ever considered how many people will be directly impacted by your death?

Make a list. Include your spouse, children, parents, or siblings and how each will be impacted, not just emotionally but financially and logistically after your death. What if your assets are frozen, your family can't find your will or your passwords, and someone has to settle your estate from another state or even another country? What if you and your spouse die together, and there is no will? What are the consequences for those who are left behind, especially your children? What if someone must try to run your business without proper legal authority? Don't you want to make solving this problem as easy as possible for them? This is truly a measure of how much you care—or not.

A second equally important question is, how many family deaths might directly impact *you*?

These might include your spouse, parents, children, or siblings. Is it possible you might have to pay for their funerals, settle their estate, raise their children, or change care arrangements for an elderly parent? It might be a sobering exercise for you actually to write a list. You can choose to discuss these situations and plan now or risk being blindsided in the future. Will there ever be a good time to address this?

According to www.estateexec.com, the average amount of time required to settle an estate is 570 hours over a period of 16 months. How would you feel about accepting this task from a family member and fitting it into your life right now? How would others feel if they had to add this task to their life after your death? Now, consider how different this task would be, with or without legal documents.

How important is it to you to be ready for a death in your family? As with anything significant in your life, you must make the time to make something important happen. When will you begin to make preparations? I hope you can now see that you absolutely do have the power to control your family's future after a death, but only if you act on it before it happens.

Become a trailblazer: Overcome the stigma of discussing death by planning for it—initiating conversations with your friends and family—sharing the results of your research—and possibly giving them a copy of this book.

Once you break through your initial initial discomfort of discussing death,, you will feel the satisfaction and relief of knowing you are doing the right thing for those you love! Now is a good time to make this happen!

Notes

Final Thought

We All Live in Denial of Our Own Death

We reside in the world of "it can't happen to me," somehow thinking that death will be delayed if we do not contemplate it. But today, approximately 9,500 people will die in the U.S., most of whom believed the same thing when they woke up this morning. It was just another day.

It is time for us to acknowledge that death is part of our life cycle. We like to have control of everything in our lives, so why don't we also want control over how we leave it? Why don't we want to consider how our death will affect our family's financial future? Why would we choose to leave all sorts of important matters in the control of others, such as the guardianship of our children, or allow a probate court to freeze our hard-earned money just when our family needs it most? Why don't we want to protect our family from the distress they will experience when a significant portion of their household income is eliminated?

Why would we choose to stress our adult children to make our final medical decisions, determine how to dispose of our assets, or even require them to pay for our funerals? Feelings of emotional loss and abandonment are expected for our family after our death, but financial abandonment is cruel and can easily be prevented or at least mitigated.

We may have worked all our lives, long or short, to take care of our families and make the world a better place, so why would we leave personal, legal, and financial chaos in our wake as we depart? Researching this book has made it clear that the most loving thing we can do for our families at any stage of life is to live the Boy Scout motto and "be prepared."

Let's not let our fear of death or procrastination in making a plan wreak havoc in our family long after we've gone. Wouldn't it be better to leave quietly and respectfully, assuring those left behind that they have been loved, well provided for, and are better off because we have lived? By being mindful, loving, and selfless, we can make this happen even if we are young and die on our way home from work tonight. Grief is a heavy enough burden for our families to bear, wouldn't you agree?

It is my great wish that you live a long life filled with love and happiness, but it is an even greater wish that when the time comes, you leave this world with a plan in place that shows your family exactly how much you cared.

Best wishes,

Clare Anthony

You are COURAGEOUS!

You tackled one of life's most uncomfortable topics!
You're definitely one in a million!

I hope you have gained new information that will inspire you to make an end-of-life plan to improve your peace of mind and provide your family with more security for the uncertainties that may lie ahead.

Thank You

If you have found this book helpful, **please consider taking a few minutes to write a review.** Reviews help other readers determine whether the content is valuable and often determine whether readers purchase a book.

As we know, the topic of death is rarely discussed. Positive reviews will increase the likelihood that this information will gain wide exposure, helping others overcome their discomfort and make plans for uncertain events in the future.

Thank you,

Clare Anthony

Notes

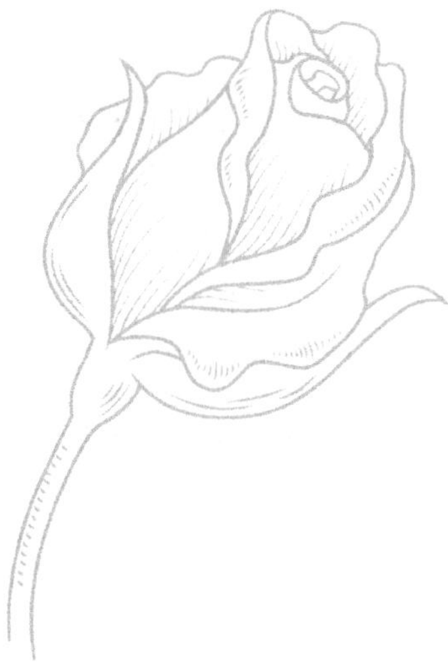

Author's Note

Writing this book has taken me in a direction that I did not expect to go, and I have followed its lead. My first goal was to write about the logistics of planning a funeral. I felt that my experience of planning hundreds of them could give people information, helping them feel less intimidated and confused after a death and thus giving them more control when they met with a funeral director. However, soon, it was clear that I needed to incorporate not only the logistics of funeral planning but also the details behind the process, so I spent almost a year researching and gathering information on all aspects of end-of-life planning.

At the beginning of the second year, another challenge emerged—the debilitating cost of a funeral. I decided to go to a funeral home and ask for a price list. I was shocked at the prices I was reading and confused by the information I saw, so I went to several more and then visited two cemeteries. It took weeks of studying these pricelists to understand how to interpret them. Finally, came the distressing moment when I realized that there was no way that the average grief-filled person could do this at the time of a death.

Searching Amazon books revealed that no one had gathered and synthesized this information and written a book on this topic, yet over 9,500 people die each day. I decided I had to figure it out. It became a challenge to break down and analyze the information I had gathered from funeral homes and, more importantly, to find a way to logically present it to an unsuspecting public. So, over the next few months, after I broke the pricing code, it became my mission to visit more and more funeral homes and gather as many *General Price Lists* as possible, soon making me question how people could afford to bury their loved ones.

This illuminated a third problem—the dangerous lack of financial well-being of over 63% of the American population who are living paycheck-to-paycheck. Entangled in these statistics was a fourth problem, the precarious lack of end-of-life planning since I found that only 32% of Americans have wills, and only about 11% have the cash in the bank to pay for a funeral. In addition, it is likely that they may not have set up beneficiaries on their accounts or investments and may not have health care directives with medical or durable powers of attorney in place. All of these factors in a single-family create a perfect storm that makes it clear that the person who dies is the lucky one.

Learning that the funeral industry is a 20-billion-dollar annual business, in some cases with a highly incentivized commissioned sales force and high-dollar marketing budgets, it became evident that reducing the cost of funerals overall would likely be impossible. However, reducing the cost of an individual funeral might be doable with some creativity and leg work. It was also obvious that the only defense for the average consumer against the high cost of dying was to make a personal plan long before a death occurred.

As an educator, I have spent part of my career helping students, young and old, reach their potential. My goal as a church musician was to inspire and comfort people through music. Now, as an author, my mission is to give you the tools to help your family walk through life's most difficult challenge—death—either yours or that of someone you cherish.

Since each death touches at least five other people directly, I sincerely hope that this book will help every one of its survivors overcome their fear of discussing it long enough to fund their funeral and make a financial plan for the lives of those they may leave behind.

If you have just suffered a death, I wish you comfort and peace during this trying time, and it is my hope that this book, *Can You Afford to Die?* will give you the knowledge you need to navigate the coming days, weeks, and months.

However, if you haven't just lost a loved one but picked up this book out of curiosity, may this, *the book nobody wants to read*, provide the tools and motivation you need to overcome your fear and discomfort with death long enough to move forward in making a plan to protect your family against life's greatest challenge.

Understand that preparing for your death and neatly enclosing it within your own life cycle is a priceless gift to your family.

Sincerely,

Clare Anthony

Appendices

While researching this book, I found hundreds of statistics. The numbers fascinated me, but I know that numbers turn some people off. So, after much consideration, I have decided to keep the statistical content and place it in a supplemental chapter in the Appendix so that the information is available to those who want to read it but not a distraction to the message and flow of the book.

Appendix A

What Are the Chances This Can Happen to Me?
The Statistics

What are your chances of a family death in the next 12 months? (2022)

Total Annual Deaths—3,273,705

Deaths of Seniors Over 65—2,509,396 (74% *of Annual Deaths*)

Total Deaths of Persons Under 64—874,333

The five leading causes of death in 2022 were:

1. Heart disease—699,659 deaths
2. Cancer—607,790 deaths
3. Unintentional injury—218,064 deaths
4. COVID-19—186,702 deaths
5. Stroke—170,000 deaths

Somewhat Anticipated Deaths

Baby Boomers—those born between 1946-1964

In 2022, approximately 2.6 million Baby Boomers died. There will be a steady rise in mortality for this group in the U.S., peaking in 2050 at about 4 million per year, gradually leveling off after 2055. The clock is ticking if you or your parent are in this age group. https://www.cdc.gov/nchs/fastats/older-american-health.htm

Cancer Deaths

Cancer is the second most common cause of death in the U.S.; 607,790 people died in 2022. Approximately 43,250 women, or 13% of the population, died of breast cancer. Other cancer deaths included lung, colorectal, pancreatic, prostate, and liver cancer.

Diabetes

Diabetes was the seventh leading cause of death in the U.S. in 2019. The estimate is that 37.3 million people had diabetes in 2021. That's 11.6% of the population. Nearly 1.9 million Americans have type 1 diabetes, including about 244,000 children and adolescents. In 2019, death certificates indicated that 87,647 listed diabetes as the *underlying cause of death*, and 282,801 listed diabetes as the *cause of death*. The percentage of Americans aged 65 and older with diabetes remains high, at 29.2%, or 15.9 million seniors, and 1.4 million new cases of diabetes are diagnosed every year.

https://www.cdc.gov/diabetes/data/statistics-report/index.html

https://diabetes.org/about-us/statistics/about-diabetes#

Unexpected Deaths

Cardiovascular disease

Cardiovascular disease has been the leading cause of death in the U.S. for the last 80 years and is the number one cause of disability. More than 800,000 people die from cardiovascular disease annually. Statistically, that is one in every three deaths. Young people are not exempt since about 160,000 of these deaths occur in people under sixty-five. https://millionhearts.hhs.gov

During the COVID-19 pandemic, the risk of both men and women dying from a heart attack doubled, likely due to people refusing to go to the hospital when they experienced symptoms, reinforcing that seeking medical attention even for vague symptoms improves a person's chance for survival.

Statistics show that one in five heart attacks is silent, meaning there is no dramatic heart pain or collapse. In many cases, the person may be unaware that damage has occurred. Some heart attacks manifest as shoulder, back, or chest pain. Other patients experience indigestion, heartburn, nausea, sweating, dizziness, or shortness of breath. Often, patients ignore these symptoms, but dismissing or delaying medical treatment can lead to irreversible heart damage.

Cardiac disease in men

The CDC reports that heart disease is the leading cause of death for men in the U.S. In 2020, one in every four men was at risk due to coronary artery disease. Each year, approximately 382,000 men die of heart attacks. www.cdc.gov/heartdisease/men.htm

Cardiac disease in women

Heart disease is also the leading cause of death for women in the U.S., killing 314,186 women in 2020, or roughly one in five female deaths. Note that one in sixteen (6.2%) of women over the age of 20 have coronary artery disease. Specifically: white women (6.1 %), Black women (6.5%), Hispanic women (6%), Asian women (2.3%). Also, 26% of women die within a year of a heart attack. Women and Heart Disease | cdc.gov

Strokes

- Strokes are the fifth leading cause of death for all Americans and the third leading cause of death for women each year.
- In 2021, one in six deaths from cardiovascular disease was due to stroke.
- Every forty seconds, someone in the U.S. has a stroke, and every 3.5 minutes, someone dies of a stroke.
- Every year, more than 795,000 people in the U.S. have a stroke, and more than 140,000 are fatal.
- One in seven strokes occurs in adolescents and young adults ages 15-49.
- Stroke is a leading cause of serious long-term disability.
- Stroke risk doubles every decade after the age of 55.
- 38% of people hospitalized for stroke were less than 65 years old.
- Unfortunately, one-third of those who have a stroke die, and another third are left permanently disabled, leaving one-third to recover.

Important note:

Patients who arrive at the hospital within three hours of the first sign of symptoms can receive a clot-dissolving drug that will restore blood flow and oxygen to the area of the brain affected by the stroke and may reduce lasting damage. These patients often have less disability three

months after their stroke occurred than those who delayed care.
https://www.cdc.gov/stroke/facts.htm

Remember this acronym

"Many people are familiar with the FAST acronym for identifying acute stroke symptoms. However, a recently expanded version of the acronym can make it easier for those witnessing an acute stroke to identify it in nearly all cases. **BE FAST** highlights two additional stroke symptoms than the former FAST acronym, making it possible to identify 95% of acute strokes, including those that occur in the back of the brain."

B — Balance loss
E — Eyesight changes
F — Face drooping
A —Arm weakness
S — Speech difficulty
T —Time to call 911

The acronym FAST was only picking up on symptoms of a stroke that occurred in the front of the brain, but the back part of the brain is responsible for balance and eyesight, and those strokes were being missed.

An article written by Kathy Morrison on May 4, 2017, in the Penn State Health News states that in the past ten years, strokes have decreased by 29% in people 65 and older. The bad news is that strokes are 44% more common in people aged 25–44. Children who grew up with poor diets, oversized portions, and inactivity are entering this age group, with some of the risks typically found in older adults. Younger people are having strokes at a higher rate than in previous years. The report indicates that even young children need to know how to recognize the symptoms of a stroke and call 911 immediately for help because their parents may be the ones having the stroke.
https://pennstatehealthnews.org/2017/05/the-medical-minute-be-fast-to-recognize-stroke-signs/

Car accidents

In 2020, there were 5,250,873 police-reported car accidents. That year, according to NHTSA, there were an average of 14,386 accidents per day, or one crash every six minutes, and 38,824 people died that year, or about 100 per day. https://www.nhtsa.gov

Domestic violence

- Over 10 million people per year are affected by domestic violence.
- Nearly 20% of marriages and domestic partnerships will experience physical violence.
- Every day, there are over 20,000 calls on domestic violence hotlines.
- 72% of all murder-suicides involve an intimate partner.
- 94% of murder-suicides involve men killing women and then turning the gun on themselves.

Three victims per day are killed by domestic partners, and 85% are women, resulting in 1,300 deaths per year. If you are a victim of abuse, call the National Domestic Violence Hotline at 800-799-7233 (800-799-SAFE) or log on to www.thehotline.org. https://ncadv.org/learn/statistics

Drug-related deaths

In 2021, drug overdose deaths in the U.S. from opioids rose to over 100,000 per year, up 28% from 2020. This includes synthetic opioids such as fentanyl and methamphetamines, as well as cocaine and prescription drug overdoses. https://www.cdc.gov/nchs/nvss/vsrr/drug-overdose-data.htm

Gun-related deaths

In 2022, there were 45,034 deaths from gun-related injuries, including suicide, homicide, and accidents, according to the CDC. There were 693 mass shootings in the U.S. in 2021, and school shootings are rising. https://www.cdc.gov/vitalsigns/firearm-deaths/index.html

Mass shootings

Death by firearms is now the number one cause of death for children and teens in the U.S., including accidental deaths, homicides, suicides, and mass shootings, according to the Kaiser Family Foundation. www.kff.org

Suicides

- Suicide was the twelfth leading cause of death in the U.S. in 2020.

- 45,979 Americans died by suicide, which is about 130 suicides per day.
- In 2020, there were also 1.2 million attempted suicides.
- The highest rate of suicide is among middle-aged white males, which accounted for almost 70% of suicides in 2020.
- 24,292 of those committing suicide used firearms (nearly 53%).

In 2020, adolescents and young adults aged 15-24 had a suicide rate of 14% of the population. Suicide statistics | AFSP

Summary

There is nothing to say after listing these statistics except that the numbers are heartbreaking. Each one of these numbers represents a family who had a personal tragedy. Many experienced a sudden, painful, traumatic, and unexpected death and had to plan and pay for a funeral in its wake. It is impossible to know how many of them are still struggling with the financial fallout that this unexpected death caused, either from the cost of the funeral and burial or from the challenges of their loved one having died without a will. My message to you is that these deaths do happen, and you can't change that, but it is entirely within your power to control the fallout that rains down on you after one of these deaths impacts your family.

Appendix B

Funeral Home Price Comparison Worksheet

Use this form to enter prices from the General Price Lists you obtain from your local funeral homes. I have included all categories to cover a wide variety of circumstances. However, to make it clear for your situation, *only enter the categories that apply to your funeral, burial, or cremation or plan.*

Cremations and Cremation Packages

Use this chart to analyze the content of the *fine print* of different cremation packages from funeral homes you visit. Use checkmarks to indicate what is included in the package and then determine if vital items are missing.

This chart can be used in two ways:

1. To compare different packages from the same funeral home or
2. To compare packages from different funeral homes.

Direct Cremation or Cremation Package

This chart will let you check off what is included in the fine print of your price list so you can see what items may not be included and will need to be purchased in addition to the package price.

You can use this chart to compare the same item, such as Direct Cremation at three funeral homes or three packages from one funeral home. For packages, you will need to look somewhere else on the GPL to find prices for missing items.

Direct Cremation or Cremation Package

Name of Funeral Home or Package			
Basic Services Fee			
Transfer of remains from place of death			
Death certificate & permits			
Refrigeration			
Transfer to the crematory			
Transfer from the crematory			
Crematory fee			
Cremation tray			
Alternative container *included or purchased*			
Cost of cremation			
Basic decorative urn			
Visitation for family 15 min			
Mail cremains for you			
Mail cremains yourself – USPS	**$30**	**$30**	**$30**
Witness the Cremation			
Urn *purchased by family*			
Total			

Prices for a Funeral with Burial

General Price List			
Basic Services Fee			
Embalming required for a viewing			
Other Body Preparations			
Casketing			
Dressing, cosmetic enhancement			
Bathing and handling of deceased			
Hairdresser			
Special care for autopsied bodies			
Refrigeration per day			
Facilities Use and Staff			
Facilities and staff for 4-hour viewing			
Funeral home use - staff for funeral			
Staff for an off-site funeral service-church, etc.			
Graveside service with staff facilitating			
After hours			
Transportation			
Transfer from place of death to funeral home			
Transfer from funeral home to place of autopsy			
Transfer to and from the airport			
Use of hearse			
Use of limousine			
Use of service vehicle			

General Price List			
Transportation outside of service radius			
Forwarding remains to a funeral home			
Receiving remains from another funeral home			
Immediate burial *(no casket)*			
Price of casket			
The Little Things			
Guest book			
Prayer cards (100)			
Thank you, cards (25)			
Musicians–vocalist–accompanist			
Clergy for funeral or memorial service- visitation, church, graveside service			
Mailing of cremated remains–by funeral home			
Mail cremains yourself – USPS	$30	$30	$30
Caskets			
Stained hardwood			
Solid oak			
Solid cherry			
Solid mahogany			
Wood veneer			
18-gauge steel			
Rental casket			
Rental casket insert			
Other			
Total			

Cemetery Price List

Name of cemetery			
Purchase of cemetery plot-lot			
Opening and closing fees			
Interment-adult-casket			
Burial of an urn-adult			
Interment of baby			
Burial of an urn baby			
Placement of an urn in a niche			
Weekend, after-hours, or holiday burial fees			
Processing fees-credit cards-insurance			
Other			
Burial Vaults			
For urns			
For caskets			
Grave liner for a casket			
Interment Options - Caskets and Urns			
Burial plot or lot			
Mausoleum			
Exterior niche marble-granite			
Interior niche glass front			
Columbarium			
Plot for urns			
Multiple urns 2-6			
Markers			
Single bronze marker 16x24 installed			
Engraving of markers or monuments			
Granite inlaid markers 12x24, 14x24, 20x28			
Headstone			
Granite			

Installation of Memorials and Markers			
Installation of memorial			
Installation of marker			
Total			

Appendix C

Funeral Service Planner

Funeral * Memorial Service * Celebration of Life

Name ______________________ Date ______________________

Location ______________________ Time ______________________

Who Will Preside? ______________________

Prelude Music before the Service *Recorded or Live–Title(s)*

____

Music to Gather *Recorded or Live–Title:* ______________________

Introduction/Welcome: *Name* ______________________

Scripture/Inspirational Reading: *Selection* ______________________

Person Reading ______________________

*Psalm: Spoken–Sung–Omit? Title*______________________

Name ______________________

Inspirational Words Clergy–Funeral Director–Family Member–Friend

____

If the service is Christian, many choose to recite or sing The Lord's Prayer

Eulogy: Delivered by: ______________________

Closing Music: Recorded or Live–Title ______________________

*****

Interment at the Cemetery (Graveside Service)

Who Will Preside?

Prayers—Scripture—Inspirational Words

Thank all who have come

Appendix D

Funeral Program Template

A Celebration of Life

Joseph C. Mann

March 12, 1972 – July 23, 2024

Insert Pic Here

Cedar United Methodist Church
Your Town, US
September 12, 2020

The Service

Prelude Music ______________________________

Opening Song or Hymn __________________ Page Number _______

Opening Remarks ______________________________

Scripture or Inspirational Reading *Reader* __________________

Remarks by Clergy or Funeral Director __________________

Song or Hymn __________________ Page Number _______

Eulogy __________________ Presenter __________________

The Lord's Prayer (Optional if a religious ceremony)

____

Closing Remarks or Prayer

____

Closing Song or Hymn __________________ Page Number _______

(Back page)

____

Please join us for a reception after the service
Interment will be at the Morning Star Cemetery

Appendix E

Common Scripture Passages for Christian Funerals

I have cross-referenced Scripture Citations from the King James Version (KJV) and the New American Bible (NAB). Included are Scriptures from the Old Testament (OT), Psalms (PS), and New Testament (NT).

KJV	NAB	NIV		Citation	Description
√	√	√	OT	Isaiah 25:6-9	God will destroy death forever and wipe away all tears for his faithful followers.
√	√	√	OT	Ecclesiastes 2:1-11	There is a time for everything under heaven
√	√	√	OT	Lamentations 3:17-26	Even from the depths of despair, God will reward those who hope in Him and await His salvation.
√	√	√	OT	Daniel 12:1-3	At the end of time, those who lived justly will live forever like the stars
	√	√	OT	Wisdom 3:1-6	The just have been tested and found worthy to rest in God.
	√	√	OT	Wisdom 4:7-15	Even a person who dies young can be found pleasing in God's eyes
√	√	√	PS	Psalm 23:1-6	The Lord is my shepherd, and I will dwell with Him forever.
√	√	√	PS	Psalm 27: 1,4,7-9,13,14	The Lord shows His path and teaches His ways for those who wait on Him.
√	√	√	PS	Psalm 63:1-9	My soul thirsts for God even in times of distress, and He has always been my help.
√	√	√	PS	Psalm 103: 8,10,13-18	The Lord is merciful and slow to anger; even though we sin, His mercy is everlasting.
√	√	√	PS	Psalm 116: 5,6,10-16	The Lord is gracious, just, and merciful; how can I repay the Lord for all He has done? Precious in the eyes of the Lord is the death of His faithful ones.
√	√	√	PS	Psalm 130: 1-8	Even in my distress and sinfulness, I wait for the Lord, for with Him there is mercy and redemption.

√	√	√	NT	Romans 6:3-9	If we have been baptized into Christ, we will be united with him in death.
√	√	√	NT	Romans 8:14-23	Those led by the Spirit have become heirs of Christ, and the sufferings of the present are nothing compared to the Glory of God.
√	√	√	NT	Romans 8:31,35,37-39	If God is for us, who can be against us, He did not even spare his own son. There is nothing that can separate us from the love of God.
√	√	√	NT	1 Corinthians 15:20-28	Death and resurrection came through a man, and the last enemy to be destroyed is death.
√	√	√	NT	1 Corinthians 15: 51-57	In death, we will be changed in an instant. At the sound of the trumpet, the dead will be raised as incorruptible and clothed with immortality.
√	√	√	NT	2 Corinthians 4:14-5:1	We know we will be raised from the dead; we are not discouraged that our outer self is wasting away, our inner self is being renewed, and we look forward to our eternal dwelling in heaven.
√	√	√	NT	John 14:1-6	Do not let your hearts be troubled; I am going to prepare a place for you; I will come back and take you with me.
√	√	√	NT	John 6:51-59	Jesus is the living bread, and he who eats this bread will be raised on the last day.
√	√	√	NT	John 6:37-40	Everyone who sees the Son and believes in Him will have eternal life and be raised on the last day.
√	√	√	NT	Luke 12:35-40	Be prepared; you do not know when the Lord is coming.
√	√	√	NT	Matthew 25:31-46	Those who feed the hungry, clothe the naked, and welcome the stranger will inherit the kingdom of God.
√	√	√	NT	Matthew 11:25-30	Come to me all who are burdened, and I will give you rest.
√	√	√	NT	Matthew 5:1-12	Blessed are those who mourn, are meek, hungry, merciful, clean of heart, merciful, and persecuted, for your reward will be great in heaven.
√	√	√	NT	Thessalonians 4:13-18	Do not grieve for the dead; those who have fallen asleep in Christ will rise to be with the Lord.

√	√	√	NT	1 Corinthians 5:1,6-10	While we are at home in the body, we are away from the Lord, but we believe that when we leave the body, we will go home to the Lord.
√	√	√	NT	1 Corinthians 4:14-5:1	While our outer self is wasting away, our inner self is being renewed. What is seen is transitory, but what is unseen is eternal.
	√	√	NT	2 Timothy 4:6-8	The end is near; I have fought the fight, finished the race, and kept the faith. I await the crown of glory.

Acknowledgments

It took a whole team to get this book written. First and foremost, I want to thank my friends Ann S. & Andre S., who helped me organize my thoughts from the very first draft. They helped me create an outline, listened to dozens of title iterations, and helped me select the cover. Andre was there every step of the way as I struggled to organize chapters, helping me to decide what to include, eliminate, or defer. He assisted with marketing research and followed this project to completion by offering contextual and organizational suggestions as he read and reread the content until I had one "final draft" after another. He gave me endless encouragement over the months, and I am incredibly grateful for his friendship and support.

I was lucky to have two career English teachers among my friends. Jane H., who read and reread the chapters over months and then the "final" draft a few times. She was there to correct punctuation, sentence structure, and content and to catch redundancies. Jane caught my misuse of the word "internment," correcting it to "interment." I appreciated her red pen, her gentle manner, and her willingness to squeeze this big project into her busy life. Thanks also to her husband, Paul, for offering computer expertise throughout the project.

The second editor was Carol S., a high school classmate who graciously accepted the position of "word smither." She was unrelenting in honing material into its most concise verbiage, eliminating redundancies, suggesting better sentence structure, and making me stick to the point, and she was a punctuation perfectionist. One of my main challenges was lists. It was Carol's suggestion to put the lists—all thirty-five pages of them–into one document for ease of editing and to check for consistency. Later, she continued to help streamline passages for flow and content. Despite Carol and Jane's guidance, Grammarly constantly undid changes that either woman offered because it could not cope with my topic, so any residual errors lie entirely with me.

A third important editor was Molly H., who had worked in an estate attorney's office. She offered admonitions against giving legal advice. She was an outstanding content editor pointing out organizational errors that might confuse readers. It took several weeks for me to incorporate all of her many suggestions. She also helped me clarify my vision for the book, which led to deferring several chapters to a second book.

At this point, I feel compelled to mention my high school English teacher, M. Davis, who is now deceased, a dedicated teacher who demanded only the best from her students. Mrs. Davis frequently tutored me in writing during my high school years. Her time and dedication gave me the foundation and confidence to pursue this project.

I want to thank my beta readers, who made wonderful suggestions and challenged sentences that I thought were perfectly clear but needed to be rewritten for the clarity of everyone else in the world. Some added chapters, some reorganized material, others challenged punctuation, but most of all, they gave me the confidence to release this book to the world. They include Gerry K., Ann S., Andre S., Vicki F., Pauline G., Molly H., Bill M., and Rose B.

Thanks also to those who shared their personal stories to give the credibility that only real people can, notably Erma A., Judith T., and several others who asked to remain anonymous. I regret what you had to go through in your experience with the death of your loved ones, but hopefully, your stories will motivate others to feel the urgency of making a plan and, more importantly, getting it done.

After months and months and dozens of title iterations, I was beyond frustration. After all, no title—means no cover design. One morning, my friend Phyllis M. called to say that a title idea had come to her. "That's it!" I exclaimed, and the rest is history. Phyllis continued to be a daily cheerleader for the project, even bringing food to ensure I was eating—that's a friend.

Then there were the investigators, Rose B., Colleen A., and Vicki F, who secured price lists from funeral homes around the country through relatives or visits to relatives. Colleen A won the prize by procuring six price lists in three different states. This enabled price comparisons to be more varied and contemporaneous from several different states. It was these real price lists from real funeral homes that verified the narrative claims made in this book.

Finally, to those who helped me select my cover design over a holiday weekend while they were traveling, preparing parties, on a family vacation, and who knows what else I interrupted. Thanks for voting not only once but three times. I am truly sorry about the timing but forever grateful for your opinions. They include Judith T., Dave S., Larry & Betty N., Jane & Paul H., Gerry K., Rose B., Pauline G., Jon & Kara B., Joanne J., and Ann & Andre S.

It takes a village. Even though I know I have written "*the book that nobody wants to read*," I am convinced that the message is important and hope it will spread from friend to friend, parent to child, or child to parent. The substance, content, and direction of the book took on a life of its own during these two years of writing, and I followed wherever it led. Consequently, the final work is quite different from the original concept. Thanks to all of you who appeared at just the right moment with the right story, comment, question, critique, or encouragement to help me move to the next step. Apologies to those of you who shared valuable stories that will have to wait for the as-yet-untitled Book II. It was painful to delay their telling because your stories were so powerful, so I promise to release the sequel soon. I truly appreciate all of you.

Clare

Notes

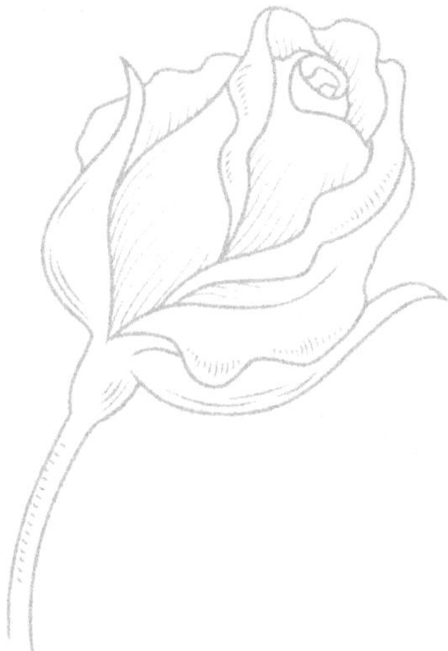

Works Cited for Further Reading

Chapter 1— Funeral-Memorial Service - Celebration of Life? Where Do I Begin?

https://www.everplans.com
https://consumer.ftc.gov/articles/choosing-funeral-provider

Chapter 2– Burial-Cremation-Donation

www.sciencecare.com.
https://www.betterplaceforests.com/blog/articles/what-religions-believe-in-cremation.
www.earthfuneral.com.
www.joincake.com
https://consumer.ftc.gov/articles/ftc-funeral-rule
https://www.ftc.gov/legal-library/browse/rules/funeral-industry-practices-rule
https://consumer.ftc.gov/articles/choosing-funeral-provider
https://www.ftc.gov/business-guidance/resources/complying-funeral-rule#the-general-price-list
https://consumer.ftc.gov/articles/choosing-funeral-provider
https://www.joincake.com/blog/immediate-burial/#: Belinda McLeod, BA Secondary Education 4/22/22
https://www.greenburialcouncil.org/cemeteries.html
https://www.greenburialcouncil.org/our_standards.html
https://www.greenburialcouncil.org/green_burial_defined.html
https://www.greenburialcouncil.org/recommended_reading.html
https://www.reuters.com/investigates/special-report/usa-bodies-brokers/
www.everloved.com
https://en.wikipedia.org/wiki/Water_cremation#

Chapter 3—Choosing a Funeral Home and the Role of the Funeral Director

www.funeralmatters.com
www.everloved.com
https://consumer.ftc.gov/articles/choosing-funeral-provider
https://consumer.ftc.gov/articles/ftc-funeral-rule
https://www.ftc.gov/legal-library/browse/rules/funeral-industry-practices-rule

Chapter 4—The Interment: Bury-Entomb-Scatter

https://www.usurnsonline.com/
https://www.dignitymemorial.com/pre-planning/funeral-costs/
opening-and-closing-fees
https://www.usurnsonline.com/
https://eirene.ca/blog/what-is-a-columbarium
www.wilbertonline.com
https://memorialplannning.com
https://www.oneworldmemorials.com/
https://Legacyheadstones.com
www.vets.gov/burials-and-memorials/preneed
https://www.va.gov/burials-memorials/schedule-a-burial/
https://consumer.ftc.gov/articles/buying-cemetery-site
https://consumer.ftc.gov/articles/choosing-funeral-provider

Chapter 5—The CHECKLIST

https://www.musicnotes.com
https://www.sheetmusicplus.com.
https://www.funeralprints.com

Chapter 6—What Are Your Rights With Funeral Homes?

https://www.ftc.gov/system/files/ftc_gov/pdf/Sample1-general-price-list_1.pdf
https://consumer.ftc.gov/articles/ftc-funeral-rule
The FTC Funeral Rule | Consumer Advice
https://www.overnightcaskets.com
https://www.titancasket.com
www.sciencecare.com

https://www.ftc.gov/news-events/news/press-releases/2024/01/ftc-sends-warning-letters-funeral-homes-after-first-undercover-phone-sweep
https://www.cnn.com/2024/01/25/business/government-warns-funeral-homes-on-pricing/index.html

Chapter 7—The Manner of Death What Happens Next

https://afsp.org/
https://www.aftermath.com/content/suicide-crime-scene

Chapter 8—Now it's Time to Plan: Will There Be a Wake, a Funeral, a Memorial Service or a Celebration of Life?

No references

Chapter 9—The Death Certificate

https://www.cdc.gov/nchs/data/nvss/handbook/2019-Funeral-Directors-Handbook-508.pdf
www.vitalchek.com/death-certificates
https://www.sciencecare.com/blog/death-certificate-need-one
https://www.cdc.gov/nchs/data/nvss/handbook/2019-Funeral-Directors-Handbook-508.pdf
https://funeralhomes.com/how-to-get-a-death-certificate/
https://www.joincake.com/blog/who-needs-original-death-certificates/ Sam Tetrault B.A. English 12/15/22

Chapter 10—Obituaries and Eulogies

www.neptunesociety.com
https://legacy.com
https://www.joincake.com/blog/obituary-website/
https://www.genealogybank.com/
www.everloved.com

Chapter 11— Planning the Little Things

https://www.1800flowers.com/blog/everyday-moments/coping-with-loss/sympathy/sympathy-funeral-etiquette-for-different-religions/

https://www.fromyouflowers.com/occasion/funeral-flowers
https://www.funeralprints.com
www.greenmeadowmemorials.com

Chapter 12—Transporting Remains

https://www.memorials.com/tsa-approved-urns.php
www.USPS.com
www.about.usps.com/publications/pub139.pdf
www.TSA.gov
https://travel.state.gov/content/travel/en/international-travel/while-abroad/death-abroad1/consular-report-of-death-of-a-u-s--citizen-abroad.html
www.neptunesociety.com
www.US-Funerals.com https://www.nolo.com/legal-encyclopedia/home-funeral-laws
https://www.insuranceiig.com/

Chapter 13—Navigating Funeral Traditions of Religions and Cultures

www.1800flowers.com
https://www.everplans.com/articles/funeral-traditions-of-different-religions
https://www.shiva.com/
https://www.everplans.com/articles/a-quick-overview-of-proper-funeral-etiquette
https://www.everplans.com/articles/what-to-expect-when-attending-a-religious-funeral
https://www.funeralplanner.com.au
https://www.umcdiscipleship.org/book-of-worship/a-service-of-death-and-resurrection
https://irp.cdn-website.com
https://www.pcusa.org
https://www.everplans.com/articles/baptist-funeral-traditions
https://www.usccb.org/prayer-and-worship/sacraments-and-sacramentals/bereavement-and-funerals/overview-of-catholic-funeral-rites
https://www.everplans.com/articles/latter-day-saints-mormon-funeral-traditions
https://www.everplans.com/articles/muslim-funeral-traditions
https://www.everplans.com/articles/anglican-episcopalian-funeral-traditions
https://www.everplans.com/articles/hindu-funeral-traditions
https://www.reformjudaism.org/beliefs-practices/lifecycle-rituals/death-mourning/what-expect-jewish-funeral

https://www.everplans.com/articles/buddhist-funeral-traditions/

Chapter 14—What is the Real Cost of Dying?

https://nfda.org/
https://www.dictionary.com/e/average-vs-mean-vs-median-vs-mode
https://www.reuters.com/investigates/special-report/usa-bodies-brokers/
https://www.ftc.gov/news-events/news/press-releases/2022/10/ftc-seeks-improve-american-publics-access-funeral-service-prices-online
https://ftc.gov

Chapter 15—How Are We Going to Pay for This?

www.cnbc.com
www.policygenius.com.
www.gofundme.com
https://ovc.ojp.gov/help-for-victims/terrorism-and-mass-violence
www.vets.gov/burials-and-memorials/preneed
https://www.va.gov/burials-memorials/schedule-a-burial/
www.lendingusa.com
www.everloved.com
www.funeralmatters.com
www.fundthefuneral.com
www.joincake.com
www.linkedin.com
www.IRS.gov http://childrensburial.org/
http://www.finalfarewell.org/
https://thetearsfoundation.org/

Chapter 16—How Bad Can it Get? Gloria's Story

www.aarpfoundation.org
https://www.census.gov/
https://ncoa.org/
https://www.prb.org/resources/fact-sheet-aging-in-the-united-states/
https://www.census.gov/library/stories/2024
https://www.ncoa.org/article/get-the-facts-on-economic-security-for-seniors

Chapter 17—Documents to Gather—The Physical, Financial, and Digital World of the Deceased

https://www.agingcare.com/articles/estate-administration-probate-after-death-in-family-153107.htm
https://www.everplans.com

Chapter 18—What Have We Learned?

www.joincake.com
https://texaslawhelp.org/
https://www.lhlic.com/

Chapter 19—Assessing Your Readiness for a Death in Your Family

No References

Appendix A—What Are the Chances This Can Happen to Me? The Statistics

https://millionhearts.hhs.gov
https://www.breasecancer.org/facts-statistics
https://www.cdc.gov/heartdisease/men.htm
https://www.cdc.gov/nchs/fastats/older-american-health.htm
https://pennstatehealthnews.org/2017/05/the-medical-minute-be-fast-to-recognize-stroke-signs/
https://www.nhtsa.gov
www.thehotline.org
www.kff.org.
Women and Heart Disease | cdc.gov
https://www.cdc.gov/stroke/facts.htm
https://www.cdc.gov/nchs/nvss/vsrr/drug-overdose-data.htm.
https://www.cdc.gov/vitalsigns/firearm-deaths/index.html
Suicide statistics | AFSP
https://afsp.org/ If you need help for yourself or someone you care about, or text TALK to 741741.
https://afsp.org/
https://www.aftermath.com/content/suicide-crime-scene/

https://www.joincake.com/blog/what-happens-when-someone-is-killed-in-a-car-accident/

https://www.pewresearch.org/short-reads/2023/04/26/what-the-data-says-about-gun-deaths-in-the-u-s

Index

Notes

Made in the USA
Coppell, TX
07 December 2025

65019593R00157